*Women Sharing Their
Mental Health Journeys*

MINDFUL HER

HANNA OLIVAS
Along With 11 Inspiring Authors

© 2025 ALL RIGHTS RESERVED.

Published by She Rises Studios Publishing **www.SheRisesStudios.com**.

No part of this book may be reproduced or transmitted in any form whatsoever, electronic, or mechanical, including photocopying, recording, or by any informational storage or retrieval system without the expressed written, dated and signed permission from the publisher and co-authors.

LIMITS OF LIABILITY/DISCLAIMER OF WARRANTY:

The co-authors and publisher of this book have used their best efforts in preparing this material. While every attempt has been made to verify the information provided in this book, neither the co-authors nor the publisher assumes any responsibility for any errors, omissions, or inaccuracies.

The co-authors and publisher make no representation or warranties with respect to the accuracy, applicability, or completeness of the contents of this book. They disclaim any warranties (expressed or implied), merchantability, or for any purpose. The co-authors and publisher shall in no event be held liable for any loss or other damages, including but not limited to special, incidental, consequential, or other damages.

ISBN: 978-1-966798-29-3

TABLE OF CONTENTS

INTRODUCTION 5

Mindful Her: A Journey of Mental and Emotional Empowerment
    By Hanna Olivas 7

Weathering the Storm: Building Resilience in Parenting and Beyond
    By Sheena L. Smith 14

Emotional Metamorphosis
    By Suzanne G Plumley 28

From Womb to Wellness: Healing Anxiety at the Source
    By Valerie Lundgren 36

Like a Whisper from the Universe
    By Pauline Grouette - Aguesse 48

From Control to Healing: My Journey Through Disordered Eating and Trauma
    By Heather Hanson 61

Silent Rage Can Be Deafening
    By Ariel Balfour 76

Divine Protection
    By Tonya Rachelle Rebhahn 90

Broken in Silence: Healing from the Inside Out
    By Melissa Cade Garcia 103

From Doing to Being: Embracing the Journey to My True Purpose
    By Aliesha Pollino 122

TODAY, WE LIVE
    By Stephanie Myers 138

From Struggle to Strength: Embracing the Journey with Compassion & Self-Care
　By Sonia Rodrigues 153

INTRODUCTION

"Mindful Her: Women Sharing Their Mental Health Journeys" invites you into a space of raw honesty, deep reflection, and unwavering strength. It's like sitting down with your closest friends, where the walls come down, and the heart speaks freely. In this powerful anthology, women from all walks of life courageously open up about their personal mental health struggles—those moments of darkness, uncertainty, and overwhelming emotion that often feel isolating.

Yet, it's not just about the hardship. It's about the triumphs—those moments of strength, growth, and self-discovery that make the journey worthwhile. Each story offers a glimpse into the resilience of the human spirit, and how, through connection and vulnerability, healing can begin. These women do not just share their stories—they extend a lifeline, offering understanding, empathy, and hope for others who are navigating their own mental health challenges.

In the pages of "Mindful Her," you'll find yourself nodding along, perhaps shedding a tear, but also finding comfort in the fact that you are not alone. Each narrative is a reminder that mental health is not a solitary battle, but a shared journey that connects us all. Whether you're seeking solace, support, or simply a reminder of the power of vulnerability, this book is a beacon of hope and a testament to the unbreakable strength within us all.

Hanna Olivas

Founder and CEO of SHE RISES STUDIOS

https://www.linkedin.com/company/she-rises-studios/
https://www.facebook.com/sherisesstudios
https://www.instagram.com/sherisesstudios_llc/
www.SheRisesStudios.com

Author, Speaker, and Founder. Hanna was born and raised in Las Vegas, Nevada, and has paved her way to becoming one of the most influential women of 2022. Hanna is the co-founder of She Rises Studios and the founder of the Brave & Beautiful Blood Cancer Foundation. Her journey started in 2017 when she was first diagnosed with Multiple Myeloma, an incurable blood cancer. Now more than ever, her focus is to empower other women to become leaders because The Future is Female. She is currently traveling and speaking publicly to women to educate them on entrepreneurship, leadership, and owning the female power within.

Mindful Her: A Journey of Mental and Emotional Empowerment

By Hanna Olivas

The world we live in today often feels overwhelming, chaotic, and sometimes, downright exhausting. As women, we juggle so many roles—mothers, daughters, entrepreneurs, partners, caretakers. We are constantly on the move, taking care of everything and everyone around us. And somewhere along the way, we forget to take care of ourselves. I know this because I've been there. I've been in that space where everything outside of me was moving at lightning speed, and inside, I was falling apart. It's easy to get lost in the busyness of life, but the most profound lesson I've learned is that our mental and emotional health must come first. And that's where Mindful Her begins.

Mindfulness has become a buzzword lately, but for me, it's much more than a trendy topic. It's been a lifesaver. It's a practice that has transformed how I relate to myself and the world around me. It's about being fully present, about tuning into the here and now, and letting go of the constant need to rush, to achieve, and to be everything to everyone. "Mindfulness isn't about doing more; it's about being more—being more present, being more in tune with yourself, and being more loving toward yourself."

I didn't come to this realization overnight. It took years of pushing myself to the brink, of ignoring my own needs, and of believing that success meant always going, going, going. I thought that if I wasn't constantly busy, I wasn't doing enough. But that mindset came at a cost. My mental and emotional health began to suffer. I found myself stressed, anxious, and emotionally drained. And that's when I realized something had to change.

The turning point for me was when I began to truly understand the connection between my mind and my emotions. I used to think that mental health and emotional health were separate entities, but the truth is, they are deeply intertwined. "Your mind and your heart are in constant conversation with one another. What you think affects how you feel, and how you feel affects how you think." When I began to embrace mindfulness, I learned how to quiet the noise in my mind, to sit with my emotions, and to allow myself the space to just be. That's when healing truly began.

In our fast-paced world, being still is one of the hardest things to do. We are taught to equate busyness with productivity, and stillness with laziness. But I've learned that "stillness is where the magic happens." It's in those quiet moments, when we allow ourselves to pause, breathe, and listen to our inner voice, that we gain the clarity we need. When we practice mindfulness, we create space for ourselves to reflect, to heal, and to grow.

Mindful Her is not just about finding peace in stillness; it's about learning to trust yourself. Trust is a big word, and for many of us, it's not easy to come by—especially self-trust. I spent years doubting myself, questioning my decisions, and second-guessing my worth. But mindfulness taught me that trust isn't something you have to earn; it's something you have to cultivate within yourself. "Trust is knowing that no matter what life throws your way, you have the strength and resilience to handle it." When you practice mindfulness, you learn to trust your intuition, to listen to your inner wisdom, and to believe that you are enough just as you are.

Love is at the core of mindfulness, but not just any kind of love—self-love. For so many of us, loving ourselves feels like an afterthought. We are so focused on taking care of others, on being "good enough" for the people around us, that we forget to show that same love to ourselves. But the truth is, "you cannot pour from an empty cup." You cannot truly give love to others if you are not first giving it to yourself. Mindfulness has taught me the importance of nurturing a loving relationship with myself. It's about showing myself compassion, forgiveness, and grace.

For years, I believed that self-love was selfish. I thought that if I put myself first, I was neglecting the people I cared about. But I've come to realize that self-love is not only necessary—it's vital. "When you love yourself fully, you show up as the best version of yourself for the people you love." Mindfulness has been my gateway to self-love. It has helped me to slow down, to listen to my body, to honor my emotions, and to treat myself with the same kindness I so easily give to others.

Mindful Her is also about reclaiming your power. As women, we are often conditioned to give our power away—to our jobs, our relationships, our responsibilities. We are taught to be selfless, to put others' needs above our own. But mindfulness reminds us that "your power comes from within." It's not something that anyone else can give you or take away from you. It's yours, and it's always been yours. Practicing mindfulness helps you reconnect with that power, to stand firmly in it, and to use it to create the life you want.

There is something incredibly powerful about being present in the moment. It sounds simple, but it's one of the hardest things to do. Our minds are constantly jumping from the past to the future, worrying about what happened yesterday or stressing about what's coming tomorrow. But mindfulness teaches us that "the present moment is the only place where life truly happens." When you focus on the here and now, you stop living in the what-ifs and start experiencing the fullness of life.

I've found that one of the most important aspects of mindfulness is being kind to yourself in the moments when you fall short. We all have those moments—when we lose our temper, when we don't meet our own expectations, when we make mistakes. And for many of us, our first instinct is to criticize ourselves, to feel shame or guilt. But mindfulness teaches us that "you are human, and being human means being imperfect." It's okay to fall short sometimes. What matters is how you respond to those moments. Do you beat yourself up, or do you show yourself grace and understanding?

The practice of mindfulness has also transformed how I handle stress. Life will always come with its challenges—there's no avoiding that. But mindfulness gives you the tools to navigate those challenges with a sense of calm and clarity. When I feel overwhelmed, instead of spiraling into anxiety, I remind myself to breathe. "Sometimes the most powerful thing you can do is take a deep breath and let go." That simple act of pausing, of bringing my attention back to my breath, has the power to shift my entire mindset. It's in those moments that I remember I don't have to have all the answers. I just need to take things one step at a time.

Mindful Her is not just about finding peace within yourself; it's about cultivating emotional health. As women, we are often told to suppress our emotions, to stay composed, to not let our feelings "get in the way." But our emotions are not something to be ignored or dismissed—they are a powerful part of who we are. "Your emotions are not your enemy; they are your guide." Mindfulness teaches us to sit with our emotions, to acknowledge them without judgment, and to understand what they are trying to tell us.

There have been many times in my life when I pushed my emotions down, believing that doing so made me strong. But true strength comes from allowing yourself to feel fully, from embracing the full spectrum of human emotions—joy, sadness, anger, fear, love. Mindfulness has taught me that "your emotions are like waves; they come and go, but you remain steady." When you learn to ride the waves of your emotions instead of being swept away by them, you gain a deeper understanding of yourself and what you need.

At the heart of mindfulness is the practice of acceptance. This was a hard lesson for me to learn. I spent so much of my life trying to control everything—my circumstances, my emotions, the people around me. But mindfulness has taught me that "acceptance is not about giving up; it's about letting go of the need to control and trusting the process of life." When you accept things as they are, you free yourself from the constant struggle of trying to make everything perfect. You learn to flow with life, rather than fight against it.

I think one of the most beautiful things about mindfulness is that it brings you back to love—love for yourself, love for others, and love for life itself. When you live mindfully, you see the world through a lens of compassion and understanding. You become more aware of the beauty around you, the small moments that bring joy, and the connections you share with the people you love. "Love is the foundation of mindfulness, and when you live from a place of love, everything else falls into place."

Mindful Her is about more than just practicing mindfulness; it's about living it. It's about making mindfulness a way of being, a way of showing up in the world. It's about being fully present in your life, about trusting yourself, about loving yourself deeply and unapologetically. It's about reclaiming your power and living in alignment with your values. And most importantly, it's about remembering that "you are worthy of peace, joy, and love, exactly as you are."

And I believe that every woman deserves that same sense of peace, joy, and balance in her life. "Mindfulness is not just a practice; it's a way of life." It's about showing up for yourself every day, being gentle with yourself when things don't go as planned, and trusting that you are exactly where you need to be on your journey.

As women, we often carry the weight of the world on our shoulders. We are expected to be everything to everyone, and it's easy to lose sight of who we are in the process. But mindfulness gives us the space to come back to ourselves, to reconnect with who we are at our core, and to honor our needs, our desires, and our emotions. "You are allowed to take up space. You are allowed to be fully present in your own life."

The power of mindfulness lies in its simplicity. It doesn't require you to change who you are or add more to your already full plate. It simply asks that you be present, that you slow down, and that you tune into the wisdom of your own heart. And in doing so, you will find the peace, the clarity, and the strength you need to navigate whatever life brings your way.

So, my dear sister, as you embark on your own journey of mindfulness, I want you to remember this: "You are enough, just as you are. You are worthy of love, of peace, of joy, and of everything your heart desires." The path of mindfulness is not about perfection; it's about presence. It's about learning to trust yourself, to love yourself, and to reclaim the power that has always been yours.

Embrace the stillness. Trust the process. Love yourself fiercely. And know that you have everything within you to create the life you want.

This is Mindful Her—your journey, your transformation, your power.

Sheena L. Smith

Certified Mental Wellness Coach & Brave Thinking Life Coach

https://www.linkedin.com/in/sheena-smith-life-coach
https://www.facebook.com/sheenazzy2
https://www.instagram.com/sheenazzy/
https://sheenalsmith.com/

Sheena Smith is an international best-selling & award-winning author, parent, educator, & Brave Thinking Institute (Dream Builder Coach).

She is the recipient of the Literary Titan book award, the IAN (Independent Author Network) Book of the Year winner for outstanding non-fiction, a Global Book Award winner for her book All Kids Can Thrive.

Sheena's adventurous spirit leads her to the exploration of underground caves, riding camels on beaches, to dancing with the Maasai people in Kenya.

Locally known as "the goat lady" for her fundraising efforts to provide goats for women in Kenya. She's also best known for her random acts of kindness & boisterous laugh.

Her mission is to inspire & empower others to shine their own light.

Weathering the Storm: Building Resilience in Parenting and Beyond

By Sheena L. Smith

Life sure can throw us some doozies! Have you ever felt that life is like a roller coaster, complete with difficulties? Have you thought it's like a relentless and seemingly never-ending storm to beat you down? How do you cope? How do you survive? What do you do when something unexpectedly pops up, when the demands of life are hard?

Life gives us all different sets of challenges. Some are harder to manage, and some are easier, but we all have our storms to get through. No one escapes this life without some degree of suffering, seen or unseen.

Whether it's a demanding job, health issue or family responsibilities, these challenges truly test our resilience and shape our future. How we navigate the storms of life is crucial in determining not only our path but the quality of our journeys.

For me, this journey has been deeply tied to the power of focus and the need to stay conscious of my thoughts and actions. It's been a learning process. It hasn't always been easy, and there were times when I felt like I had no choice but to push forward. I discovered that mindset and the things we choose to believe in play a crucial role in our ability to overcome adversity.

Many times over the years, people have said to me, as a mother of children with special needs, "I don't know how you do it." My thought has been, "I don't have a choice." That is where you push through as a parent who unconditionally loves their children.

This sentiment has encapsulated so much of my journey, especially when I think back to the days of raising my family. One of the most profound moments in my life was when my daughter was born prematurely with the unexpected complication of spina bifida. At that moment, it didn't matter what challenges we would have to face. All that mattered to me was that she lived and would have the best life possible.

I remember standing by her incubator, holding her tiny hand and praying for her health and her happiness. All I wanted was for her to live. Have you ever been in that situation? Praying for your child's survival and life? It truly is a traumatic experience because, inside, you are falling apart and trying to appear strong and supportive on the outside. Another heart-crushing experience I remember vividly is when I had to hand my child over to a nurse to be prepared and sedated for surgeries. It made no difference if it was dental work or back surgery. Any surgery was equally traumatizing to me as a parent.

Through the years, not only was I balancing raising children, including two with special needs, but I also had the responsibilities of working full-time and running a family and household. It was not easy at the time. I had two older children who were active in hockey, which meant juggling trips between two different arenas and two different towns. My spouse works long hours, often leaving me to manage things on my own. The daily routine was exhausting, but my commitment to my children's well-being kept me going. I am grateful for the days when he could be there to help. He has always been my rock, especially since our two with special needs were born. He was always first to step in and help. Learning about the medical issues that a child with spina bifida has, gave him the confidence to help with her needs. Knowing how to care for our daughter's back, and measuring her head hourly to ensure that everything was draining well to prevent hydrocephalus was paramount. The need for an eight-hour drive to the hospital, or the thought of an emergency flight for surgery added to the stress. Thankfully, we got through that experience without the need for that surgery.

Despite the constant demands, I learned to find strength in small victories, whether it was managing to get everyone to their activities on time or simply making it through the day. Those moments of perseverance became the building blocks of my resilience. I remember the days of having a crazy schedule. I worked full-time, oversaw the opening of the new kitchen at a local hospital located an hour away, and still had to ensure everything at home was running smoothly. My day began at 4:30 AM and involved getting my two oldest children (they were 15 months apart, and it felt like I had twins at the time) to the babysitter before embarking on my 45-minute drive to work. The routine was grueling: work a full day, return home, wash bottles, pack bags, do laundry, prepare meals, give them baths, feed them supper and collapse into bed. More often than not, it was alongside my children, only to wake up and do it all over again.

Winters were even more brutal. Often, the water was frozen. I'd have to spend time blow-drying the pipes under the sink to get running water so that I could wash my face. Many days, I wasn't successful. I'd have to wash my face, brush my teeth, and throw on some makeup at work. The wood stove would be out, and the house would be cold. I'd load my two babies into sleeping bags and take them to the babysitter so they could continue sleeping while I drove to work for my 6 AM start time.

This routine left little time for self-care or reflection other than on the drive. Sometimes, I was just too tired to even think, I was so sleep-deprived. There were many nights that I would just crash on my kids' beds with them in my arms.

Our house was old. We had a granary, and when we shipped the grain, the rats came into our house. I know, disgusting, right? I didn't discover that until the night I took out a loaf of bread from the freezer to thaw for the morning to make some sandwiches. The whole loaf was gone except for the empty bag. There was not even a crumb inside it. It was then I realized that we had rats, so I went to buy a rat trap at the Local Co-Op. They handed me a little tiny mouse trap. I said, "No, bigger!" They gave me a really big mouse/rat trap, and I took it home to capture the critters that terrified me. The thought of them in the house made me fiercely protective of my kids. I was sure the rats would come into their beds at night. See what happens when you let worry get the best of you?

Through those years, survival was truly my only mode. I felt like a rat running on a wheel, round and round. Those days left me exhausted from constant stress. It was taking a toll on my mental health. Burnout wasn't just a concept for me. It was my reality daily. My mind and body were screaming for rest, but I felt trapped by the demands of the circumstances. I had health issues myself as a child and was diagnosed with juvenile arthritis. I lived with pain daily. I could feel my health getting progressively worse, both physically and mentally.

Growing up, the conversations around mental health were nonexistent, almost taboo. Yet physical activity was encouraged. People rarely talk about their mental well-being. As an adult, I began learning to be conscious of my thoughts and finding out about the power of focus, I started to recognize that, despite my thoughts, I might have had signs of anxiety, ADHD and depression. I often felt sad, fatigued, changes in appetite and disrupted sleep patterns. However, I attributed those symptoms to my situation rather than acknowledging them as possible mental health issues. In reality, it could have been a combination of everything going on in my life and my coping skills.

Years ago, when I was feeling overwhelmed, I found myself crying in the doctor's office when he offered medication. I declined, believing that my depression was situational. I thought if I could just change my circumstances, I would feel better. I didn't realize at the time that my mental health needed attention just like a physical ailment. I wasn't open to medication. I preferred the natural route.

I began learning different strategies to cope with my experiences, and I learned the importance of cultivating a growth mindset by focusing on positive thoughts and actions. I could navigate through life's challenges more effectively. It didn't mean ignoring the difficulties, but rather choosing to focus on solutions and what was within my control. So much of it was not in my control. During this time, I experienced the death of a loved one, so I had to learn how to grieve as well. Grief and coping are a whole other story for another time.

As an empath, I find that I pick up on the energy of people around me. If someone is sad around me, I pick up that energy. For example, I walked by this person in a bookstore in Toronto. I was in a good mood because that's my happy place, being in that bookstore, with so many books to choose from! This woman walked past me, and instantly, I felt sad. I turned around and looked at her and said, "Are you OK?" She burst out crying and said that she was new to Canada and was feeling very lonely and sad. We exchanged emails, and I was hopeful that I possibly made her feel better. I went on my merry way, shopping for personal development books by my favourite authors.

Another time I was having a massage. I went in there in a good mood. I know that people process feelings when getting treatments, but I was still in a good mood. The next thing I knew, I had tears rolling down my face. The masseuse was by my shoulders, and I said, "Are you OK?" He said, "No, my boss just gave me trouble." He continued, " I feel terrible." Again, I tuned into the feelings of someone's sadness. It's happened many times throughout my life. I feel that I'm very sensitive to the sad side of others, maybe because of my sadness.

I'm not sure if it's a cellular memory thing. I also believe that you can carry memories through your ancestors. I feel like there were times that my mother and maybe her mother had very sad times, and that possibly I carry that sad sensitivity. I am not sure, but I know that I need to focus on positive thoughts, positive feelings and a growth mindset.

Learning how to build on these skills has been quite the journey for me. Mindfulness practices have become a cornerstone of my mental wellness routine techniques. Exercises, like deep belly breathing and four square breathing, help me manage my feelings of anxiousness. Incorporating gratitude daily into my life, and taking moments to appreciate the small joys has become a powerful tool for shifting my mindset. I also enjoy EFT (Emotional Freedom Technique). It was a relief to learn how to ease stress and induce calmness quickly. I often teach this valuable skill to my students.

At bedtime, I listen to manifesting videos as I fall asleep. Alternatively, I love to listen to rife frequencies. I found them on YouTube. You can search for whatever you're looking for help with. For example, I search for 'rife' and 'nausea' if I'm not feeling good, and quite quickly and surprisingly, I feel better. I feel that the rife machine is one of the greatest inventions of all time. I wish the benefits were more widely known. Perhaps one day!

I do know that the future of our wellness, physical, mental, and spiritual, will be in our own hands. The more that you know to help yourself, the better. There are many tools for that, such as the few I've mentioned throughout my story.

Another one of my favourite tips is expressing gratitude daily by taking moments to appreciate the small joys. It has been one of those powerful tools. Before I go to bed, I like to think of five things that day for which I am thankful. I'm developing the habit of writing down those five things as a new routine this new year. In addition, each morning, I say, "Thank you for this day." I often add, "Show me how I may serve today" because I love helping others feel better.

Continuing on my journey of self-care, I had learned the hard way, that neglecting my needs for so long had led to burnout, headaches and chronic pain. It wasn't until I started prioritizing my well-being that I began to see improvements. Simple practices like spending time in nature, ensuring adequate sleep, eating a balanced, protein-rich diet, omega-3 fatty acids, whole grains and fresh fruits and vegetables helped me regain my energy and mental clarity. In addition, I found nutritional supplements that got to the true root cause, which was a true blessing.

Despite becoming a Certified Nutritional Consultant, until then, there was still a piece missing in my wellness plan, so my search continued.

Recently, I discovered the missing piece. If you are suffering in pain and not finding answers, if you feel like your health is getting worse each year as you age, know this is not your fault. It could be your gut. Discovering the link of the gut/brain connection was a game-changer for me. Realizing that the health of my gut directly affected my mental health encouraged me to make better nutritional choices. This included taking quality, strain-specific probiotics, prebiotics, phytobiotics and nutrient-rich foods. My diet became a non-negotiable part of my self-care routine.

I recently became a Certified Mental Wellness Coach because I learned the value of getting to the cause of gut health, and I wanted to help others. Science is beginning to show the correlation between mental health, gut health and brain health. They're all associated. If you have an unbalanced microbiome, health problems can become systemic throughout your whole body. Indigestion, headaches, inflammation, heart problems, brain fog, hormonal issues, lack of energy, belly fat and bloating are only some of the symptoms you might experience.

I've known for a long time now that nutrition is important, but I didn't understand the role the gut plays with cravings. This makes it difficult to change eating habits. I consider myself an ex-chipoholic I'm in recovery. I love chips, and I would eat them off a conveyor belt if I didn't end up suffering afterwards. The salt content and seed oils lead to indigestion and inflammation, which leads to more pain throughout the whole body.

You require resilience when you're weathering life storms. My strategies for resilience have become my lifeline during the most challenging times. It's the ability to adapt and recover in the face of adversity, and, for me, it's a skill I had to cultivate intentionally to navigate raising four children (two with special needs), managing a household and holding down a demanding job. It taught me that resilience matters. Self-care is not a luxury; it's essential. You need quality self-care to have the strength to endure, recharge and go through life. I discovered that resilience is built through small daily actions and maneuvering successfully through tough times. Each time I was faced with a new challenge, whether it was a medical emergency with my daughter or a financial setback, I learned to approach it with a mindset of perseverance and positivity. I remind myself that storms eventually pass, and this difficult moment will, too. I remember my dad saying, "Things always work out. Maybe not the way we want them to be, but they do work out."

With a growth mindset and emotional regulation as my tools for staying grounded, I thrived.

Noticing and mindfulness have become the most powerful tools in my mental wellness tool kit. By staying present and aware of my thoughts, feelings and emotions, I can prevent myself from spiralling into overwhelming anxiety or stress. I look for good in any situation. Sometimes, it's hard to find it, but it is there. When in a state of overload or overwhelm, I seek solitude to contemplate my thoughts and responses. Without doing so, I know I might say things that I'd regret. I don't stay mad, so taking time to process the experience allows me to move on.

When I practice emotional regulation, I gain understanding. I then can manage my emotions rather than letting them control me. It allows me to respond versus react, meaning I can consider how to address what's happened and gauge the outcome before taking action.

Other techniques that help me are journalling to process my feelings. Noticing what's going on around me and being aware of my feelings helps me gain clarity. Gratitude helps me shift my mindset and change my focus from what's wrong to what's right. There is good in everything, so look for the good. I like to say to friends, "What's new and good?" It's easy to focus on the bad, but sometimes, what's new and good is where the focus should be. It creates good energy, and energy is everything!

I consider myself a loner. I love to spend time by myself to reflect and think about things in life. It gives me a perspective on how to solve my problems. I love to sit by the water, alone with my thoughts.

Another key aspect of resilience is knowing when to lean on others. For a long time, I tried to do everything on my own. I believed that asking for help was a sign of weakness, but I learned that building a network of support through family and friends was essential for my mental wellness. I'm a work in progress, learning to lean on others and ask for help. I'd always had the mindset that if I asked for help, people would let me down. I believed I would be told no, and that would be devastating. So, as a fiercely independent person, I don't often rely on others, but I've learned to ask when it's important. An example is asking a friend to review the chapter you are reading. She is so smart and knowledgeable (and so cute and funny) when it comes to proofreading. She's always willing to help me when she can. I am grateful for her. Thanks, Peggy! We get by with a little help from our friends.

Having people talk about their burdens with me and seek advice made a significant difference for me. It reminded me that I wasn't alone in my struggles and that it was okay to rely on others when needed. I also realize that many people go through similar things. It's good to have conversations with others who are on the same journey as me, whether it's parenting, personal development, nutrition, or the mental wellness industry.

Mental wellness can be a balancing act when you're juggling responsibilities. Life as a working mother, especially one raising children with unique challenges, is a constant balancing act. It requires juggling multiple responsibilities and making sacrifices. I often felt stretched in trying to be everything to everyone. However, there came a time when I realized that maintaining balance also meant setting boundaries and knowing when to say no. I'm pretty good at saying no now, but it's taken some time, and it took a toll on my health before I learned it.

When I face times of grief or when my boundaries are disregarded, I tend to turn inward, feeling deeply saddened. I appreciate and value clear communication. So many of us were not taught how to communicate effectively. I've had to learn this as well for the sake of my boundaries, my peace of mind and my energy.

I'm still a work in progress. I'm learning to prioritize tasks, do the things that matter most first and delegate when possible. I've learned to accept that I can't do it all and that my well-being is just as important as my family's. This shift in perspective has allowed me to manage my time better and avoid the burnout that has plagued me for years. Sometimes, many of us are busy because it's an avoidance tactic. By staying busy we avoid the decisions and the things that we need to do. Be mindful of why you do what you do.

The experiences of life and juggling responsibilities of working full-time and raising children, doctors' appointments, educational appointments, travel to specialists, financial issues, etc., I found myself in a constant state of dysregulation. My cortisol was high. I constantly felt the need to be busy. I didn't know what it was like to sit, be still, and be calm. I had to learn that. Where are you in this process? Are you keeping yourself too busy? Are you experiencing overwhelming overload? What are you doing for your self-care? What are you doing for your mental wellness?

Did you know that mental wellness is not a destination, but an ongoing journey? It's about continually learning to adapt and finding a way to support your mental health and emotional health through the years. I've discovered it's okay to stumble and face setbacks. What's important is to keep moving, seeking growth and healing. I often say to others—rest but don't quit. Whatever your goals are, keep going for them. Sometimes, people think when they're not reaching their goals that it's not meant to be for them. They believe that they're not meant to have financial freedom or they're not meant to have good health or they're not meant to have peace or they're not meant to have whatever their goal is. But the truth is, it's about comfort zones. Learning and doing what it takes to move beyond your comfort zone is what helps you reach your goals.

My journey has been about more than surviving. It's about thriving despite the challenges. I've come to appreciate learning resilience. I feel the tools I've gathered and the mindset I've developed are only part of a process that continues to evolve, but one that makes me stronger and more capable of whatever life hands me.

How resilient are you? What strategies do you like to use?

Resigning and quitting doesn't make you stronger. Resilience is like muscle, the more you use it, the stronger you become. One vivid memory that stands out is the time my daughter had to undergo major surgery. The anticipation, fear of the unknown and sheer worry of the situation were overwhelming, but resilience taught me to take one step at a time. I had to focus on what I could control and trust in the process.

Additionally, you build resilience by setting small achievable goals during tough times. You break down overwhelming tasks into manageable tasks and celebrate small victories along the way. This approach can help you keep momentum with a sense of accomplishment. If you are grieving, you take things one day at a time, one hour, one minute, one second at a time. Whatever you can do, you do what's best for you. There are no set rules for grief.

If you can stay mindful, positive and emotionally regulated, it helps you to be grounded. It helps you to feel calm amid chaos. I recall a time when everything seemed to be going wrong, appointments were running late, the seemingly endless demands of life piled up, and I felt on the verge of breaking down. I took a moment to sit quietly, close my eyes and focus on my breath. Breath is our strongest and best technique. I played some music, and, in a few minutes, I felt a sense of calm washing over me, reminding me that I could manage whatever was dealt to me.

During the years of raising kids, I remember having some crazy mornings. I'd be fighting with kids to get up, get ready, pack their lunches, pack their school bags, get the clothes on and get out the door. In my rush and distraction, I'd hit the garbage can as I was backing out of the driveway. Many days, I had to remind myself to stop and breathe.

Techniques like deep breathing, doing a body scan or mindful walking can help you stay present and reduce stress. Start these exercises with short sessions and gradually increase the duration until they become part of your routine for mindfulness. Try to build up to 20 minutes a day.

Move your body as much as possible. Walking in nature is so good for you, and stress is released by a moving body, so shake it off.

I also suggest people do this: put your hand on your heart and ask yourself what the most loving thing you could do at this moment and then do it. Time management is a tool that has helped me as well. I like to time block my day and my week so that I can be organized and focus on goals.

The journey towards mental wellness is an ongoing process. Like the storms of life, the journey can be filled with highs and lows. Each challenge can teach you more about yourself and show you where you can improve and grow and learn to make yourself a priority.

After years of neglecting self-care, I made it a priority to carve out time for activities that rejuvenate me, such as reading, journalling and simply enjoying a cup of coffee. Spending time at the park on the waterfront, walking, taking in the fresh air, riding my bike and, more recently, learning somatic yoga are some of the things I enjoy and make time for.

Make self-care a non-negotiable part of your routine and schedule time for activities that nurture your body, mind and spirit. Personal self-development has helped me be stronger and more resilient. I've learned the techniques, strategies and tools from leaders such as Bob Proctor, Dr. Wayne Dyer, Louise Hay, Napoleon Hill, Marci Shimoff and Debra

Poneman. I love their wisdom on how to live a life of abundance and happiness.

I hope that these tips, tools and strategies will help you with life's challenges, making you stronger and more resilient. I hope you feel unstoppable as you go for your dreams. They're waiting for you because they're already inside you. They are waiting for you to breathe life into them.

Suzanne G Plumley

Enriching Lifestyles LLC
Coach & Sole Prenuer

https://www.linkedin.com/in/suzanne-plumley-1a8773129/
https://www.facebook.com/groups/675129774822445
https://www.aspiebridgebuilders.com/

Suzanne Plumley, a certified Life Coach will help Late-diagnosed Autistic women design and manifest a life in harmony with their Soul's purpose.

Suzanne started her career as a classroom teacher, but realized that her true heart was in enrichment programs that allowed children to find their true interests and gifts. Her current interest is working with LD Autistic women become knowledgeable about their diagnosis so they can create a joyful and spiritual life.

She shares her journey of her Autism late-diagnosis in three chapters of a book collection called Short, Sweet, and Sacred. Utilizing her pen name, she authored Five Simple Rules: Christian Guide to Dating about Autism relationships.

As a life coach and professional speaker, Suzanne offers an inspiring vodcast with colleagues offering transformational topics to help clients gain new solutions to life challenges. Her signature non-profit program, Aspie BridgeBuilders, connects clients with coaches in their zones of expertise.

Emotional Metamorphosis

By Suzanne G Plumley

Imagine a world where you are completely on your own in your most authentic version. While you have a "family," they are not with you but rather on the side of society that refuses to change their perspective on disabilities. They see that people who are different from how they behave are bad or have serious problems. They watch television through critical eyes and make fun of or ignorantly comment that a person or a character that looks or behaves in a peculiar way is not someone for whom they can see any positive traits.

Many people say that family is your strongest support system that you can count on, but I have repeatedly seen the opposite to be true. Family, when they can accept each member to be their authentic selves and empower each member to live a life that they choose without regard to its impossibility due to personal constraints, can be a strong support system. They can rise and stand behind celebrating their successes, but also be a soft place to land when an endeavored activity fails to meet expectations. There is no, or very minimal, competition among its members, nor is there favoritism or higher regard for a particular member, and thus more empowerment and resources are provided. Instead, on the flip side, I repeatedly heard that life is not fair.

My family would not believe I was disabled as it would have been a reflection, they believed, of themselves. Instead, they wanted to believe that the diagnosis I did receive was responsible for all indifferent behavior. To this day, my late diagnosis or a new explanation for my behaviors is denied, and yet, at the same time, they are angry when a trait under that diagnosis shows up. They are quick to tell me that I must change that trait to be more in conformity with their family system of values.

A strong support system is exactly what I would have loved to receive in my life. While it was a challenge to go into society with their misunderstanding or ignorant generalization of what autism is, they would not have been the issue in my life had I had the support system at home to counteract their belief system. However, I found myself in the position of being alone on one side of the tug-of-war rope with my family and society on the other side.

* * *

I am autistic, and while other women would not start or even say that aloud or in print, I have come to learn that understanding who I am authentically has been a euphoric experience. Of course, not every woman is autistic, but very few will pull back her layers to really understand how or why she behaves in a particular way. They will often say to themselves, "As long as I am not sticking out in the crowd, being too showy or rude, or even showing up as a wallflower, does it really matter who I am?" My answer to that question was a definitive YES! I needed to know why I was bothered by social injustice or intolerance of rule breakers, one of the traits that an autistic woman may experience. I had felt different all my life and struggled to understand why I was not fitting in or feeling like other women who can show up looking like they were all put together from confidence to stilettos at the interview or a social gathering. I was not looking or feeling the part of what appeared to me to be a "successful woman," and today, I am perfectly, well, perfectly happy accepting my role in society.

I was born back in the sixties, long before the word "autism" was a term in the medical, psychological, and educational fields. Even today, there is still scrutiny for each woman who starts to understand herself through a self-examination of behaviors that look quite different from siblings, early classmates, and now colleagues as well. So many of us were measured by the typical growth milestones that every pediatrician was taught to analyze, but these were not behavioral or psychological tests, but rather physiological ones such as growth charts and motor skill development. Once we entered school, the intellectual factors started to be assessed as part of our development, such as school readiness, letter recognition, and math and science basic skills of shapes and sizes. However, social development in terms of expression of thoughts, social interactions, or a deeper level of communication skills. While some had advanced progressive reading skills and understood math skills, little concern was placed on internal behavioral needs, and thus, they were considered on track by educational assessments; others who could not quickly pick up these skills were called delayed, and at the most insufficient level of advancement, these children were "mentally retarded," and a label of deficiency was slapped on some. I "squeaked" through the call for help as I was able to read books leveled above my grade level and thus considered on track even though I would go out for recess and retreat to a book to avoid the harsh teasing of my high voice or incoordination of motor skills.

Co-existing medical conditions were often the leading diagnosis of children who were not progressing on the milestones in relation to their siblings or other children at the same age level. This was the case with me as I was born without a working thyroid which meant that I was diagnosed with hypothyroidism. There was a gross misunderstanding that the underworking thyroid, even with proper medication, was not only responsible for the metabolic system but also caused all my behavioral challenges, such as meltdowns and schoolyard fights when someone cut the four-square line. These challenges were considered unruly behavior when I tried to leave my book on the sidewalk and get involved in recess. In the current organization I am now involved with, it was a call for help or loving attention if the meltdown occurred at home, but the call, often ignored, received no concerned attention.

When a medical or psychological problem exists and members of the family do not explore the root causes of the challenges, it can be neglectful, and thus trauma is caused by invalidation and gaslighting;

now compounded post-traumatic stress disorder is an additional problem for the woman to surmount on top of the undiagnosed autism. I was fifty-one years old before an organization realized that my traits showed up as possibly being associated with autism as experienced by the behaviors of a family member diagnosed at an early age.

Fortunately, the trials I faced with two advanced brothers as unwanted competition did have a positive aspect that can help other women now if they are willing to appreciate their authenticity. From an early age, I learned the value of determination and perseverance to compete against the woman I was yesterday. However, it took me a long time to realize these truths about how my determination and perseverance could be two of my best traits to triumph over the difficulties I faced until learning I was autistic.

My greatest burdens took place just after my divorce in 2014 when I had the strength to look at my life and realize that I no longer needed to be stuck in a life of being "less than" my husband; eventually, I learned that that marriage was only the mirror image of the family I grew up in with their views that I was not as smart, athletic, or successful as my brothers would be as adults. This time of greatest struggle lasted ten years as I realized who my enemies and my allies truly were, who I could unconditionally count on in good days and hard days. I learned that although a set of people were my family, they were not necessarily the ones who would have my back on the days when I needed the most support. They were there when it seemed that they could hold their truths and strength over me; and, later, I learned that money was the transaction for this permission to control my life decisions. These were the hard years of seeing the Truth of my power versus being blissfully ignorant that family was the set of people upon whom you could always count. I remember the hardest month of my life when a principal, who couldn't trust my differences, forced me out of my position as a substitute teacher and would bend the truth to keep me out of teaching children in other districts. The great stress of losing not just my substitute position but also the realization that the school allowed a false accusation of hitting a child on the to block me from all teaching positions. This mind fog caused me to make a bad driving decision that resulted in a hydroplane across southbound traffic struck by a Mac truck and a minivan. My strong belief in angels, and no near-death experience, saved me from certain death. Getting on my knees and asking my God what was next for me put me in the place to receive a podcast from a woman who would lead me to my chosen family. A loving organization that would accept me for who I was and help me to become aware of exactly who I was going to become.

While I heard the woman on the podcast, I would soon learn just how very loving and how much of a spiritual leader she was to serve thousands of people who experienced similar trauma that I did, as well as deathly illnesses, broken marriages, and other life-defining moments such as my ended career and hydroplane accident. I went to her conference feeling as though I was wearing a full suit of armor, as I was afraid to trust people who didn't understand me. I was still trying to fit into a neurotypical world unknown to me that I had been living on the Autism Spectrum all my life. I joined her organization as a client to learn how to rise above all the conditions and situations that had brought shame and feeling like a victim in my family of origin and my divorce. I had been experiencing depression from those situations and had gone to eight years of therapy with four therapists who never recognized the autism, only the codependent traits that followed me from the way my mom had treated me and into my marriage. The program that the woman on the podcast taught seemed to erase in six months what pains I endured through a mind-fogging prescription and therapy. I was elated to finally live in the truth of my potential instead of in victimhood.

Each month spent in class brought in a new strength within me that I had never experienced before, and the rest of the organization gave me a sense of belonging that I had never received. In addition to the class, there was a program to learn how to become a spiritual transformational coach, and after seeing the strength in myself through the positive energy emitted from the teacher and the community at large, I very much wanted to share these experiences with other women who were now living on the level I was living. At first, upon completion of the certification and examining the ways that I could best serve others, I learned that in the age of technology and personal phones, people had stopped caring about the language they were using around loved ones as if they were strangers on the street, so I made it my mission to be a coach of positive, supportive language that incorporated breath work and a pause before speaking to loved ones or reacting to what they were saying.

However, within the year and a close study of my behaviors around others, a member of the faculty approached me to inquire if I might have received an autism diagnosis. I was euphoric! There had been many years of not understanding why I behaved in certain ways was having a negative effect on how I was received by others. With the assistance of my PCP, I went through a two-and-a-half-hour analysis to confirm my diagnosis. Autism without intellectual deficits, formerly considered Asperger's Syndrome, and now autism level 1.

Late Diagnosis Autism is what can save a woman from searching for ways to combat shame and victimization caused by a family system that neglects her true needs and considers the mistakes she makes as bad decisions, not traits of autism. They try to control her future because they are unaware of how to truly help her thrive in life. This is how I turned my corner, but not without the great pains of misunderstanding my true needs. I realized that my mistakes caused by a lack of unconditional love and supporting the challenges of life could have helped me thrive. I could have benefited from the diagnosis of autism in girls while I was still in my early school years to receive important life resources just as the girls who were born after the year two thousand were discovered early in life.

If I can put into mindful consideration that every day I can be a better version of myself, then I can beat the limiting beliefs that a woman can beat the victimized trap in which she feels trapped by family and society to rise above those conditions caused by shame to live among society most authentically. Will it be easy to navigate in a world that does not yet fully understand autism traits and levels of challenges, no, but if she can learn to utilize determination and perseverance to live according to her core value of authenticity, she can rise to accept herself and all the gifts she has been given and reduce the pain associated with people who may never completely understand her. We need to live with the belief that we need to accentuate our positives to live our best lives and stop worrying about the people who are ignorant of our gifts.

Valerie Lundgren

Mindful Wellness
Holistic Health Coach & Reiki Practitioner

https://www.linkedin.com/in/valerie-lundgren-70570a37/
https://www.facebook.com/lundgrenmindfulwellness
https://www.instagram.com/lundgren_mindful_wellness/
https://www.mindfulwellness.me/

I am here on this earth to empower women who are struggling with anxiety and overwhelmed with emotions. I created a specialized program using Reiki, Hypnotherapy and other holistic and clinical modalities to equip you with tools on your journey of healing. You have the power within to heal, I am here to guide you on that journey.

After the birth of my son, I struggled with anxiety and later developed Melanoma. This shook me to my core - knowing I needed to make some changes, I embarked on a spiritual journey to help my body heal. As I began to discover my potential to heal, I hungered to gain the knowledge to help others. As a holistic health coach and Reiki practitioner, I teach you to take the power back into your hands. I will personally guide you to making simple health-promoting adjustments that produce real and lasting results.

From Womb to Wellness: Healing Anxiety at the Source

By Valerie Lundgren

My mental health journey began in the womb. (Though truly, it may be traced back through many lifetimes, let's focus on the impacts in this lifetime.)

I was conceived about two months after my brother had tragically passed away. He was three years old when he died. My sister was nine months old at this time as well. He died from a terrible, tragic accident that left him in a coma for three days. After three horrible days on the ventilator, my parents had to make the most difficult choice a parent would ever need to make, and said goodbye to him.

While in utero, I was absorbing and taking on all of my mother's pains, fears, and worries without her knowing. Imagine the pain, sorrow, and fear you would feel as a mother after your child tragically dies. I also had a traumatic birth coming out—the cord was wrapped around my neck.

So, why do I share all of this with you? The traumas we face in utero and childbirth can affect our whole lives without us really knowing until we have an "awakening" of sorts.

I discovered my core wound of anxiety in this lifetime stemmed from the womb. It all began with the death of my brother. I was not born yet, but I was conceived months after his death, in profound grief and pain. Of course, my parents loved each other, but unfortunately for me, they were both mourning their child who tragically died. They were also having feelings of fear—fear of life, fear of death, fear of this tragedy befalling their other children. My mom, as she carried me, had felt all of these emotions, and I took on these in utero. I subconsciously adopted beliefs of being unworthy of life and constantly fearing death. Fear became my operating system.

It was a set belief of mine. Not feeling worthy of life and being scared of death. I remember being a nervous child. Not wanting to be home alone. I wasn't a huge fan of sleeping over places. I wanted to be home. Home was comfort. Home was safe. I grew up like most children in the 80s. Working parents, latchkey kids. It was odd in my house; I felt like I was watched like a hawk. Some of my memories were of me, being alone, for hours, and at such a young age doing things I couldn't imagine a child doing today. Like wandering near a river, walking to a shop downtown at age 5. I can remember my fears from childhood so intensely. There was a time when my grandfather drove us up the side of a mountain in the Black Hills. I was in the fetal position on the bottom of his Suburban, crying and pleading to go back down. Heights, going fast, being alone, turtle necks, scarves, enclosed spaces, too many people... they were all too much. All of these fears came from a place of not feeling safe in my body. Some of which were again from past lives, I later came to find out, but they were amplified and on display in this lifetime. This was my lifetime to start the healing process.

Through my teen years, I didn't know what anxiety was. I had no idea what being an empath or psychic was. This was all so overwhelming to my already taxed nervous system. I could feel the breakdown. So, I started drinking and using drugs. This was my escape. I thought it would make me feel "normal," but instead, it opened Pandora's box. My panic attacks increased, and I was losing control of my life. During this time, my father was battling his own demons and was going through alcoholics anonymous. This was my wake-up call as well. I knew I had to change my way to start healing. I didn't really know what I was going to do, I just knew I had to stop with the drugs and alcohol, or I was going to end up worse than I was. I was married after high school and had a child just a few years later at age 21. I was so excited to become a mom. Unfortunately for me, this is where the anxiety went to the next level.

My awakening came after the birth of my own child over 20 years ago. I remember the evening of my first panic attack like it was yesterday. I could feel my heart clenching like a vise. My heart was racing, faster and faster, like a horse being shot from the gates. I could feel the sweat starting to drip from my arms and the dizziness... I couldn't keep my head straight and feared I would fall over. I was in my rocking chair, watching the Oscars, the award for best costume design had just been announced. I was breastfeeding my son at the time. I remember getting up from the chair and shaking uncontrollably. Going to the bathroom, feeling like I could lose it from both ends. I first thought I was having a heart attack. For those who have had panic attacks, you know what I mean. You fear the heart racing and lack of oxygen is going to kill you. I made my way to the bedroom to lie down, going back and forth in my mind if my husband should call an ambulance. He came in to comfort me and to try and calm me. It took several minutes, which felt like hours, before I could finally breathe normally again. I can only remember fragments now from the rest of that evening. I know I eventually fell asleep and can only imagine it was a tough night of rest. When I woke up the next day, I called my doctor and made an appointment to see her. At the appointment, she confirmed that yes, it was a panic attack, and had prescribed me Xanax. I was very reluctant to take this pill. I had my child, so naturally, I didn't like taking medications of any sort. So, why would I take this? I feared the side effects would be too much for me. So, how am I going to fix this? I can't be a functional mom with panic attacks. Can I?

Postpartum anxiety wasn't widely discussed then. We hear about postpartum depression, but anxiety often remains in the shadows, and back then, it was not very well-known at all. I now know that giving birth was a "trauma" on my body that awakened the anxiety I had felt during the time I was in utero. It created a "spark," one that needed attention; my smart body was saying, "Now it's time to heal," but I was not listening. I kept pushing it down, covering the symptoms, ignoring the "elephant in the room."

As the years progressed, the panic and anxiety became more severe. I knew I had to figure this out. So, I started researching, digging into the why, and how. Wanting to understand these panic attacks. I felt crazy at one point. Like, maybe I should be in a facility. This can't be normal? No one else feels like this. I was also so ashamed. I kept it hidden pretty well from family, friends, and work. I just pushed all the worries, fear, and anxiety down further. I felt like I had to put on a brave face while I was crumbling inside.

I am a holistic/naturalist type of person, so I first went to see an acupuncturist. My first session was very profound, I had a very deep healing and even saw Jesus during my first session. I kept up with these sessions for a couple of months. My panic started to reduce and was much more manageable. Although I still had anxiety, at least the panic attacks did not affect my daily routines.

Well, that wasn't the case for very long. I can remember still going and doing things with the family, like flying to Seattle (I had always had a fear of flying but seemed able to do it just fine, even with the panic attacks), going on trips out west, and going to family functions. I say this now because, in only 10 years from here, I was unable to do these things.

Through the years, my panic disorder and anxiety would come and go; sometimes, it was worse than others, but it was manageable. Seeking relief, I turned to holistic methods: essential oils, energy healing, exercise, yoga, some natural herbal remedies, and Chinese medicine. All of which seemed to keep things moderate and at bay.

What really brought the panic disorder overboard was when I decided to open a gift store during the recession. (Yeah, really smart.) I had no savings and no credit, and I just went for it. The man who owned the building we were renting from financed the start-up of my business. So, I was finally living my dream. I had gone to school for business, I worked at a retail shop on the main street and I knew this was what I was supposed to do with my life. I was good at it, too, we doubled our sales every year, but unfortunately, I wasn't ever able to pay myself, we were bleeding money. (Oh, and did I mention two months after we opened the store, my husband was let go of his job? So, yeah, things were tight and tough!)

I can remember the stress of running this business, the one that I thought defined me as a person and was my purpose in life. Every day, I would stand behind that till and feel my heart race, my mouth dry up, and I would be so dizzy I would have to sit down. My legs would shake, and my arms were weak. I could barely get through the day. In fact, there were days

I had to close up early, I couldn't be in this panicked state anymore. I wish I could say that when I returned home, I felt better, but that wasn't always the case. The anxiety followed me everywhere, like a bad smell you can't escape from. Anxiety and panic started to come back in full swing and were now impacting my daily life and routine. So, what do I do? I work harder, work two jobs besides running my gift store, drink more caffeine, eat more sugar, and eat more junk. How I thought this was going to help is beyond me. So, here I go, burning the candle at both ends and not finding any time to really stop. The anxiety and panic kept getting worse. And amidst all of my own anxiety, I was also dealing with my children's anxiety. Both of my children had absorbed and inherited my anxiety as well in utero. Watching your child struggle with anxiety because of you, and you are unable to manage your own and feel regulated to assist them, was like a non-stop cycle of fear. I was starting to have issues driving, being in stores, going to public events. There were many times I would have to pull over when driving due to the panic taking over. I couldn't see straight, my heart was racing so fast that I couldn't breathe to calm myself. I started avoiding places because of the panic. I was struggling with my new job, working within the schools. There were days when the panic was so bad, I would be shaking and dizzy, but have to fake my way through the day. I started making myself sick. Because being honest that I was having panic attacks was not enough. It wasn't excusable from my family, my job, and all of society, really. I actually became sick, so I had a legitimate excuse. One that I would actually garner sympathy for. I couldn't attend family gatherings or make it to work very often, my immune system stopped functioning at full capacity. I would be sick almost every month. Sometimes, it was the immune system not working, and sometimes it became psychosomatic, where I would actually make myself sick to avoid situations. I missed almost every family gathering for about eight years; to this day, I still miss family gatherings that are not near me. The disappointment from others and lack of empathy still hang on my heart today. I wasn't doing any of this on purpose, yet I was treated like I needed to just get over it and move on. Like, there was a light switch I could just flip, and voila. Life was back to normal... I really wish with all of my being, it was that simple. I still struggle with being in a car for long periods of time and being far away from my home. I wish I could give you a miracle story of complete healing, but this has been a slow process, one that has taken longer than I expected, and I have now honored the pace as it is. So, with all this struggle comes more struggle. After four years of running my body in complete stress response daily, I developed cancer. I had gone in for a mole removal because my mother had pointed it out one day. I still remember her words very clearly. "I don't like the look of that one, you should get it removed." I was like, well, umm, ok? It looked normal to me. When I arrived at the doctor's office, I had my four-year-old with me at the time. As we waited for the doctor, I started to feel nervous. She greets me, checks the mole, and says, "We need to do punch excison." Oh, so not just skim it off and go, now I need a bit more extensive removal? She takes me to a surgery room with the kiddo in tow and has me lie on a bed. She injects my chest area with a numbing agent and proceeds with a punch removal. Think like a paper hole punch but for your skin. She stitches me up and sends me home.

A week later, I got the phone call I had been dreading... "You have melanoma." What? I was shocked, stunned, scared, and mad. The dread and fear of death came over me. The fear of death that had loomed over me since childhood became visceral. Was this it? I was scheduled for surgery to do tissue removal of the area to see what stage I was at. I have never had surgery, so I did not know what to expect. Well, being uninsured, I was awake for it, and they did the worst job ever of retrieval. I felt like I was at a butcher shop, I can still smell the burning flesh as the surgeon was cauterizing my flesh. After this surgery, I waited in pain and fear for over a week to receive the results of the pathology test. Finally, I get the call; it is a level 0. All cells were removed during the punch excsion. Thank GOD! But of course, it doesn't stop there, monthly appointments were made for the dermatologist, where they continued to remove moles that looked suspicious. All have come back Atypical- but not of concern. So, I continued on with dermatology appointments, making sure the cancer was never coming back. The stress was still there, I was running a store that was losing money, working two jobs to keep it all afloat, and was not addressing the real root cause of my panic and anxiety. As I continued to push forward that year, another huge life event shocked our world. My brother-in-law Joe had committed suicide. He had struggled with his mental health since he was a young boy. He and I would always rely on each other for support and help during mental health crises. Although his pain was deep and hard to manage, we really were not prepared for this. You always have the reflective "what ifs", and "if only I had done XYZ." How could I have helped him and prevented this from happening? Our family home was the hub that evening for all to mourn in shock, pain, anger, and sadness. It was a very heavy time for us all, especially the children. My own kids were 8 and 10, their cousins were 10 and 12. So painful for them to process. Still to this day, they are processing it all. Suicide leaves behind a stain on your heart forever, the death hits harder. As I am writing this I just caught myself holding my breath. Exhale...

At this point in my life, all was crumbling down. I had started taking care of my body before Joey died. I was starting a meditation practice and self-hypnosis. I was just starting to find some calm and was going to share it with Joey, but I was too late.

When I started my healing journey, I was alone. I had the support of my husband, but I was alone. I had no idea where to start or what to do. I couldn't really find anyone similar that could relate to these feelings. I kept signing up for classes/courses that were promising quick fixes, getting rid of anxiety for good. These promises of not having to live this way were so enticing. I kept going for these quick fixes in hopes that one would work. Nothing was really working. There were times when I had thoughts of ending my life. Not that I really wanted to end it, but dang it, this constant battle raging in my body was exhausting.

Having the frustrations from family and friends coming at me did not help. I shut down even more. Only my husband understood. Only he got it.

It took time, but my family started to get it, too. I had to be able to explain it to them, and at that time, I really had no idea how, either.

The best way I could explain what I was going through was this story.

A woman breaks her leg: she can't get to functions, can't drive, and really has a tough time doing much at all. She needs to rest, to heal her leg. We give her grace, support, and love because we can all understand and relate in some aspect to her broken leg. I had a broken leg, but no one could see it. I needed care, love, and support. Not criticism, frustration, and resentment. Care for me like you would for a person with a broken leg.

This also sparked a passion in me to share my story. Finally, I became brave enough to admit who I was, who I am, and who I wanted to be. I was then able to share my story. I want to end the stigma around anxiety and mental health. I don't want others to feel ashamed and ostracized like I had felt. I want those that have anxiety to stand proud and tall, to feel empowered! To know that no matter what, they are loved and supported!

That is why this book means so much to me. Mindful Her is all about breaking that stigma barrier, and empowering women who are struggling with their mental health, they are not alone, and they are loved. Knowing that other women are just like you and have almost the same stories gives you hope and encouragement. I also love that my business is called Mindful Wellness, it just fits so well into this book.

I could hear the victim part would come forward and say, "Why me?"

But as I have learned through my healing journey, "Why not me?" was more appropriate. This was my wake-up call, my chance to start some really deep healing. Not only generational but past life!

I started with meditation. I took a meditation/mindfulness course which opened my eyes to a whole new way of living. I went deep down the rabbit hole and started doing self-hypnosis. I got into several self-help gurus online, bought books, listened to podcasts and courses, and took educational courses on anxiety. I wanted to learn all I could about it. The why, how, when. As I became more educated, I started to implement new healing modalities. I had discovered there was no "cure" or "quick fix" for anxiety or mental health issues at all. I had gone for years hating myself, hating anxiety. Cursing it daily.

I started to connect more deeply with myself, understanding more about the nervous system and what I truly needed. I went to school for health coaching. There I continued my education with whole body healing. It was through this program that I had my "aha" moment with anxiety. We must look at the whole body for impactful and long-lasting healing. I started shifting my diet to eating healthier, more fruits and veggies. Taking the right supplements, focusing on gut health (did you know 90% of your serotonin is produced in the gut?). I also let go of this notion that I needed to be "fixed" or that anxiety was a curse. I came to love my anxiety. I no longer was fighting it and becoming angry at it. I look at anxiety like a child. It comes to you screaming, and acting all crazy because it needs your attention. But when you meet that child with the same energy of frustration, you will only both be worn out and nothing will be resolved. When we approach our anxiety with love, compassion, and empathy, we find it calms much quicker. It truly just needs space for us to feel the emotions and space to relax the nervous system. Our anxiety is a signal that we don't feel safe in our bodies. To remedy this, we need to make it feel safe. And giving yourself love and acceptance allows space for safety. I focused on mindfulness and meditation, exercising for the first time in my life and practicing self-hypnosis, therapy, energy healing, herbal supplements, and really doing the deeper, harder inner work I had avoided for so long. I started healing and reducing panic attacks daily, down to weekly, down to monthly, down to ever so often, all with the focus of connecting more deeply with the thing that scared me in the beginning. I now have respect for my body, love for my body, and compassion for my body. I understood why she was trying to protect me for so many years. It is now time for me to give her attention, respect, and love.

With all the modalities I had learned, schooling I took, and mentors/healers I met through the years, I created a specialized coaching program specifically for women who are struggling with anxiety, self-worth, direction and purpose, and connection with self. Within the three months of working together, we meet weekly for coaching and an intuitive reiki session. We work on your healing goals each week. During these three months, we look at nutrition, hormones, gut health, meditation/mindfulness, and how to incorporate it into your daily life with ease, TimeLine Therapy©, Hypnotherapy, and Re-wiring the brain to what you truly want in life. This intensive program is for those who have done therapy or are in therapy and are looking for something a bit more, a little extra nudge to really open them up to finding themselves and having a deeper healing connection. This is my passion; I want to help other women become empowered and feel the way I do today.

Coming to acceptance of what and why has allowed me to be me, I now love myself more than ever and make no apologies for who I am. It took me a long time to get here, though. If I could recommend anything to those who are struggling with anxiety right now, don't give up. Each day will be difficult, some are better than others, but none are a waste. Start small, with even just moments of mindfulness. One mindful tip I will leave you with today that you can try yourself this week; take a mindful minute break to stare out a window. Look at nature for one minute. Focusing on a tree, a bird, a flower, or a blade of grass. Just breathe as you bring awareness to whatever you are looking at. When thoughts start flooding your brain, just redirect and focus back on the subject. Breathing in and breathing out as you focus your attention on nature for one minute.

Pauline Grouette - Aguesse

Founder of Guided Journey Coaching

https://www.linkedin.com/in/pauline-grouette-11a8ba216/
https://www.facebook.com/guided.journey
https://www.instagram.com/guidedjourneycoaching
https://paulinegrouette.com/
https://www.guidedjourneycoaching.ca/

Like a whisper from the Universe

Join me as I share my story of resilience, mindfulness, and self-discovery, guided by my own intuition, like a whisper from the Universe. I learned to navigate the waters of the dental industry with ADHD, and as a single parent. This chapter has been brewing in me for decades.

Being an Alchemist, mindfulness extends to my 1:1 clients and motivational speaking, where I empower clients to unlock their true potential. As a Reiki Master and dedicated mindfulness student, I aspire to teach, while continuously expanding my knowledge to include CBT and Emotional Intelligence. I am honored with the esteemed title of Canadian Ambassador for LOANI and recognized as a Top Awareness Coach in 2023 by IAOTP.

Driven by an unwavering commitment to making a difference, my non-profit organization, Proud Pathways, is dedicated to supporting children and single parents. Listen to your inner whisper!

Like a Whisper from the Universe

By Pauline Grouette - Aguesse

Have you ever really thought about mindfulness? I had heard the word before but never really gave it a second thought, probably because it was as foreign as feelings, and connectedness to myself and my soul. This was part of the whisper that I kept ignoring because I was so disconnected. In my opinion, family stories, traumas and chains had to be either broken or reinforced in order to help my present family and future generations. While growing up, I was often told to be careful and to think before speaking. I learned to adapt as I stumbled through childhood, misguided teenage years, and very angry early adulthood. There was a lot of confusion as I tried to sort it all out. I put mindfulness (with a high probability of ADHD) in a box and hid it high up on a closet shelf, so I didn't have to think about the possibility of something more being wrong with me. Growing up with abandonment issues was very real for me until, one day, I decided to leave my dental assisting career of 23 years in order to sort out disconnectedness in my family once and for all. Becoming mindful was something I challenged myself to learn as I took that Pandora's box off the closet shelf and looked to see what it revealed.

I loved learning how things worked, and how to build and do things on my own. This is when the whispering began. I instinctively knew that I had to learn life skills in order to become the person that I longed to be. I remember adults often pointing out the valuable life lessons. Hearing how important it was to learn to survive in this uncertain world was valuable. I felt like I had to become resourceful as a child in order to gain respect from the adults around me. I often felt as if my comments were contradicted because, in school, I was encouraged to ask questions, though when I asked questions at home, I was told things were none of my business or I would say the wrong things because I was messing facts up in my head. This is where I learned a strong limiting belief in my family: I was not good enough to ask questions, and "working hard was necessary just for survival." Forget about even thinking that dreams could come true! That's why they were called dreams. I was told they were not real. Growing up in the 70s, it was common on the weekends to leave the house in the morning and come home when the street lights came on. My vigilance was astute, and I learned to navigate situations by watching other children, teens, and adults navigate situations. Perhaps this inner voice was determination and courage. I believe now that this inner voice or intuition was guiding me to start paying more attention to the whispers.

My mind was always so busy that being told to stop and slow down seemed like I was setting myself up for failure! My grandmother would tell me to "...slow down and smell the flowers," and would often ask why I was in such a hurry. Slowing down made me feel anxious. I thought that if I slowed down, I would miss out on something fun or an opportunity to learn something that could help me fit in. I didn't realize it at the time, but she gave me my first mindfulness lessons. In university, I would try to bring books to the dinner table so I could read or study, making the most of every minute I had. Being the headstrong teen that I was, I didn't want to admit she was right. The words that I read were not retained, and I found I had to read them repeatedly, and still, the words would not always be understood. She taught me that I was not really retaining anything because my mind was too focused on the food. In order to help my body and mind connect (and avoid getting a sore stomach), tasting the food and imagining it going to my stomach slowly helped, so I felt more satisfied when I focused on eating and slowed down. I also felt full with a smaller portion. Another bonus was that my mind could focus on what I was reading afterwards. I needed to nourish my body so it would stay strong and healthy. I felt slowing down prevented me from working hard, but I had this wrong.

I learned early to listen to family stories so that I could learn from my ancestors. As I became a Mentor for everyone around me, I realized in my forties that I was a people pleaser. I wanted to be liked and feel important, so I would help everyone else before I helped myself, which often led to my needs getting pushed down further and further. This created deep feelings of not being as important as everyone else around me. This held true, especially in my dental career. As a dental assistant I was very passionate and wanted the office I was working in to be successful. I didn't realize that I didn't need to sacrifice my boundaries or beliefs simply because I was working for someone else. I could still be respectful and professional, by creating an atmosphere where everyone still felt welcome. A problem when I first started in the dental field was that I was not connected with my feelings or myself. I was in the middle of divorce proceedings, working full-time, and was the sole provider to my three children. On top of this, there were extracurricular activities, like swimming, hockey, Cub Scouts, and Brownies. I understand now how my ancestors became disconnected from themselves in order to survive the traumatic events that occurred in history, depending on the role they played, for example, during WWII. In some situations, they could only think of survival, and it was to kill or be killed... Literally, this was my paternal side. In other situations, they had to do as they were told and not ask questions. This was the situation on my maternal side, the total opposite of Dad's family. Life was very confusing to me.

The biggest confusion to me was not knowing my paternal family. My paternal family was very entrepreneurial and very different from the traditional agricultural family that my maternal side presented to me. I never knew it at the time, but it was as if the whispers were preparing me to one day meet my paternal side by developing my entrepreneurial skills and becoming the leader I was meant to be. I longed for the paternal connection deeply, and the Universe knew the answers. The Universe encouraged me to join certain clubs like Girl Guides or 4-H, where I stayed for seven years, eventually becoming the Club President. I was always active, whether in sports or groups that could enhance my future professional career, like becoming the high school yearbook editor. This experience taught me how to lead a group of people towards a common goal for the school to enjoy decades later. At the same time, I helped plan the graduation celebrations. The Universe kept whispering in my ear to follow certain paths like getting a post-secondary degree to help whatever career path I chose. As a teen and young adult, it was common for me to have many projects started at one time, and to be on at least two committees, on top of full-time school or work. I felt the need to keep myself occupied so that I could avoid the huge void that built in me, creating an even greater disconnect between body, mind, and soul. At the time, I didn't realize that this avoidance was my reality and that ADHD was greatly a factor until everything came to a halt in my first year of university, and I came face to face with it.

There were many events that I blocked out as a child because the trauma was too horrific for me to acknowledge, and I hadn't the foggiest idea of how to process all of the emotions that started to surface. My stepdad and mother lied about my dad wanting to be a part of my life. The lies accumulated until I was nineteen years old when I found out my biological father's name, and that he was close to where we lived. My grandfather sexually abused me from the age of 10–14 years, and my mother didn't believe me. My stepdad continued to tell more lies because he needed me to help with the business he purchased, which was barely staying afloat. At this point, the lie he told was that when he adopted me, he swore to keep me safe like his own daughter. I just found out the truth at fifty-three years old because I had to renew my passport. So many lies were told to keep me away from who I really was that the emotions led to suicidal ideations.

This is where the whispers from the Universe saved my life. I still did not know how to process these big serious feelings, and I felt that there was no way out. I felt confused, angry, frustrated, and alone because I had no one to talk to and thought no one would understand. I was so embarrassed and let pride take over. I had never felt so alone in my life. I felt like there was a huge black hole where my heart used to be. For months and months, I would strategize how I would end my life. When the Universe whispered this time, it was different; now, there was hope. What kept bringing me back to the reality that I was important and meant to do something big was my paternal nudge, like a whisper sending hope that one day we would connect. Universal energy is all around us. This is a proven fact!

One day, I knew that I would be reunited with my paternal family, and they would be proud to welcome me as their own. I started to speak to a counselor, and she helped me discover the little girl who had been abandoned by the people who were supposed to love and protect her. I started to rediscover who I was, and I began reconnecting with the girl I once was. There was no happiness, but a lot of sadness and longing to be loved as the little girl she was. Scared and naive of the world that her parents never explained to her. Slowly, the doors began opening in my mind with my soul, which was my deep inner being, or inner child. I started journaling to deepen this connection and let my inner child know that she would never be alone again. We had a lot of work to do, beginning with love and trust for each other.

The connection of body, mind, and soul is important for mindfulness and healing. Even though I had the best intentions, I am human and made many mistakes. Someone came into my life that I was not expecting. This relationship was very toxic, and the strength that was gained had again been put on a shelf. I birthed three children and dedicated my life to them. I promised them that they would never have to experience the same loneliness that I had. Ancestral healing is important because, in epigenetics, we have learned that it is not only the physical features that are passed through familial lines but also the personality traits. Women in my family on both sides suffered much abuse and rape by men who dominated them in toxic relationships as depression and ADHD sunk in their grasp further. I realized that in order to break these chains that held down the women in my family, I would need to be stronger and more courageous than I ever had been. This was the only way to deeply heal these generational wounds that I intended not to pass on to my children, but unintentionally I did. I was focused on saving my family. All of my family, which included those who came before me, but first I needed to be present in the current situation. It seemed like overnight, I became a single parent of three, working in a position that would not support my young family to the extent that I wanted to. I never wanted them to feel alone, to go without basic necessities which included being able to go on school field trips. I will be forever grateful for those parents who saw me struggle and stepped up to help with clothing donations, rides to shared team sports, and finances, so they could feel as if they belonged. I wanted my children to be proud of the hard work I did; they were my priority as I placed that little girl back in the corner… again.

When I decided to shift my career from hospitality to the dental field, I felt that this was exactly what my skills as a supreme organizer and multitasker were for. My children were six, three, and two years old when I went back to school. I lived and breathed dental assisting, and I took my children on this passionate journey with me. I learned right from the beginning that in order for a dental office to operate effectively and efficiently, all staff members needed to work as a team. This exposure to a new level of professionalism was everything I had hoped for. All team members had an important role, and by being partnered with great dentists, I could continue my sponge-like quest for knowledge. I was a zealous supporter of my dental patients and the field in general. I learned everything I could to expand my knowledge and serve my co-workers, patients, and colleagues even greater. My success was the success of the office, or so I thought.

I never considered at the time that the owner was making the money, it was their business, not mine. For the first decade of my career, this didn't bother me because they encouraged me to work overtime (at the same rate hourly, not overtime pay as per the Manitoba Labour Board.), sacrificing my family time, and doing what I could to save the office money so the bottom line would help everyone. I worked outside of my scope of practice by cleaning toilets and emptying trash bins to save the office the expense of hiring a cleaner.

I always had to summon up the courage to ask for a raise. I was very grateful to be working in what I felt was a prestigious field, and how dare I be selfish in asking for a share of the money I had saved for the office. My self-esteem was low, and I learned how to wear many masks to keep my position. I felt important because I was helping people build their self-esteem by assisting them in creating beautiful smiles. I felt the need to go out of my way for the office to have a successful appointment, which led to a successful day, then a week, then a month, and so on, and eventually, I felt I would get recognized for my hard work. I would have almost stood on my head if they had asked me. I volunteered as the tooth fairy because I loved seeing the children's faces light up when they saw me. I felt invincible being able to help change by-laws and contribute to decisions being made, so the public no longer saw the negative stereotype that dentists are only in the field for the money. I volunteered on the Manitoba Dental Assistants Association Board for six years, so I could understand how the innards worked between the dentists and the assistants. There were some offices that were disrespectful and even unethical, and I wanted to help make things right for my fellow colleagues. I strived to be the best Dental Assistant that I could be. For the first time, I felt valued and that I was meant to be exactly where I was meant to be, regardless of the sacrifice I was making financially and energetically. I became a multi-tasking queen in the dental field, as so many assistants do.

Even though I was very productive, I was not working to my full potential because of multi-tasking.

Today, being mindful consistently reduces anxiety, enabling me to make more sound decisions and finish projects on time, in a much more fulfilling way. I learned that when I slowed down, I was able to complete whatever task it was more completely because I would not forget any steps, or try to take a shortcut. Getting the task done mindfully was NOT what was causing my angst, as I initially thought; it was my lack of attention to the task. The end result was filled with more love and intention and was ultimately stronger than when I wasn't focused.

Society and technology have led us to believe that we need to do many things at once to become the supermom or the dynamic employee. The reality is that all of those tasks that I was more mindful of gave me a sense that I did a better job because they were completed to a higher standard of care, and to the absolute best of my ability at the time. Before, I would often feel that sigh of relief because I got something finished, but was I deeply proud of it? In full transparency, not really. I was letting myself down because, according to social standards, titles and accomplishments are how people judge your worth. This was why I felt the need to be on so many committees, yet also to feel that I was giving back the generosity and the kindness people had shown me while raising my children. Robin Sharma's *Leader Without a Title*, explains this best as he speaks of ordinary people, doing ordinary tasks, but the difference is the growth inside. Having extra letters before or after your name, like Dr. or D.M.D., to show your achievements is ego-based. This is not authentic, nor is it fulfilling in the big scope of life. Achievements for the cause bigger than you while remaining humble are authenticity deep in your soul. This was the book that really shifted my mindset.

It was not easy to step out of my comfort zone by walking with fear rather than allowing fear to lead me. I had to start re-evaluating my habits and start taking accountability for my mistakes. I allowed myself to think back to when I became an adult by Canadian laws when I turned eighteen years old. When I was allowed to make decisions that affected my life as an adult, the real lessons started. I consider life up until that point as preparation for the challenges that were to come. Three marriages, three children, two divorces, near-death experiences, and consistent whispers from the Universe that led me to my paternal family are where I landed. After the children graduated high school, I made the conscious decision to make changes to my life that I felt had been put on hold while I raised them to the best of my ability. Part of those challenges included forgiving myself for the many times that I could have been a better parent or partner with family and friends. I had to put those times into perspective of the environment at the time where I was in life. I also had to remind myself that I am human and it is okay that I made mistakes. I consider those "mistakes" lessons that I needed to learn in order to become a better person.

I wish I could say that those lessons were full of greatness, but that would be a lie, and I will take off my rose-colored glasses for you. As a senior assistant, I am not proud of the way I treated some of the new graduates while they were still learning the ropes and navigating the waters to go from classroom to full-time dental assistants. The two weeks that we perform as part of our practicum in order to graduate are almost like a job interview, though it still does not prepare you for the reality of the real world, at least mine didn't. When I did my practicum, it felt like a dream and wasn't real because I was overwhelmed with everything else going on in my life. I was a single parent, going through a divorce, and I was full of anger and resentment. I brought this energy to the offices that I worked in, though I didn't realize it at the time because I was so disconnected from myself. I didn't dare take that box off the shelf in my closet yet. I needed a job that could support my family, so I put on the mask that so many of us do, and I continued to push those feelings down rather than process them. As the years passed in my career, there were times when I would erupt because that box had become too full. I was impatient and controlling and would raise my voice unnecessarily at work and with my family. Taking responsibility for these actions required forgiveness and reparation for the many relationships where I was not my best self.

Apologizing to the assistants who were in similar situations as I was, as a new grad, was part of my first steps, though again, allowing myself to reflect on the environment I was in at the time, needed to be considered. I realized that I could not be fully to blame as some offices took advantage of my situation, enthusiasm to learn, and naivety. I had not started my deep healing until a few years before COVID-19 started in 2019. In 2016, I recognized that I needed to start taking steps towards being the person I strived to be. All areas of my life were affected: my health, my relationships, my career, my finances, and my spiritual beliefs. All of these areas were challenged! I was presented with the hard choice of looking in my mirror and letting go of the toxicity that was around me. I started to form strict and respectful boundaries that I had not existed before as a people pleaser. As a result, I had to accept the relationships that I would lose. The relationships, that I thought were supportive. I learned that when I started to respect myself, the people who were meant to be in my life for genuine love, and respected me for who I was, came back into my life. I held myself to a different set of standards now, and it did not go unnoticed. One person who I have known since I was a teenager actually asked if I was on medication because I had changed my mindset and demeanor and grounded myself so drastically. I chose to be the person I am today, and this is how I did it.

Slowly, I started to feel the benefits of slowing down and taking time for myself. There were many new practices that I started, like meditation, and I started to educate myself on self-care. A well-known Zen saying,

"When you drink, just drink, when you walk, just walk."

I started to listen to guided meditations daily. The guided meditations helped me to focus on the words that the guide was saying. I focused on the tone, the music, if there was some, and the words, which activated my imagination of the world that had been closed off since childhood. I took online courses in CBT (cognitive behavior therapy), and read self-help books like *The 5 AM Club* by Robin Sharma. He had a 90-day guide which helped me revamp my morning and evening habits. My world started to change in such welcome ways that I felt like a sponge again! I joined a fitness group that encompassed fitness, nutritional eating, journaling, and meditation. This group formed a huge part of my life! I met ladies from all over the world who provided a safe space where we could relate to our daily life trials, joys, and tribulations and also encourage us to get back up when we have fallen. I learned about grief, guilt, love, forgiveness, and gratitude. I learned in a simultaneous instant as I began with this group that I needed to leave behind my old ways and fully surrender to what may be presented to me. I learned the difference between superficial surrendering and a deeper spiritual surrender. Only when I surrendered the control of my life and fully began to trust in the Universe, did I meet my husband and soulmate.

I realized that the Universe had my back and had been with me all along. I was so busy living according to what I thought was normal in society, simply so I could fit in. Everything that came into my life once I got rid of the barriers opened doors to opportunity. I gained the courage to walk with fear, which brought abundance, acceptance of my ancestors, and an understanding of the life challenges that had only encouraged me to be stronger and braver than I ever had been!

The whispers, also known as my intuition, were with me all along and brought me the abundance, love, and freedom that I had always desired. Mindfulness, along with the other practices that I introduced to myself, allowed me to be less anxious and bring more peace to my life. I learned to work with the undiagnosed ADHD that I had on the shelf in a box, deep in the closet. I learned to process the emotions head-on rather than avoiding them. I continue to try not to procrastinate which only provides distraction from being present in the moment. There will always be personal growth as I create the new identity of the person I want to be. I am very realistic, so I have also learned that even though 70% of mental health issues can be worked with, I now see that medication is sometimes helpful. In order to become the person I know

I always had inside, I will be mindful of any diagnosis that may come.

My takeaway message to all of you reading my chapter is to let go of any attachments or judgements that you may have of living your life to the fullest. When you breathe, close your eyes and use your imagination. Inhale through your nose for three seconds and exhale out of your mouth for five. Allow your mind to go blank as you follow your breath. Allow yourself to feel the air go throughout your body. Start with five minutes as you feel your body relax, and slowly increase this time for yourself.

I am grateful you are here.

Namaste

Heather Hanson

Flourish Nutritional Therapy Consultant
Gut-Brain Wellness Expert

https://www.linkedin.com/in/heather-hanson-870752b1/
https://www.facebook.com/flourishntp
https://www.instagram.com/flourishnutritionaltherapy/
https://flourishnutritionaltherapy.com

Heather Hanson, known as the "Gut Health Paramedic," is a best-selling author, speaker, and wellness expert with over 26 years in healthcare. She is celebrated for her transformative Digestive CPR and Mindset Revive frameworks, which empower women struggling with bloating, fatigue, brain fog, and weight gain to reclaim their health through a holistic approach. Heather's passion stems from her personal triumph over autoimmune thyroid disease, driving her to uncover root causes of health issues. She combines expertise in digestive health, hormone balance, detoxification, and mindset to help clients achieve cellular-level healing. Through her personalized coaching, speaking engagements, and writing, Heather inspires others to see symptoms as messages from the body and provides clear, actionable roadmaps for lasting transformation. Her mission is to help others break free from health struggles and embrace a vibrant, confident, and energized life.

From Control to Healing: My Journey Through Disordered Eating and Trauma

By Heather Hanson

"Trauma isn't just in your head. It lives in your body. Healing begins by understanding and releasing it."
– Author Unknown

Words I Wish I Could Tell My Younger Self

Dear Heather,

I know you feel ugly, unlovable, and not enough. You think that if you were thinner, prettier, or more "normal," maybe life wouldn't feel so hard. Maybe you wouldn't feel so broken.

You tell yourself lies like: *You're damaged. No one will ever want you. You'll never be enough.* And slowly, those lies take over, chaining you to a cycle of shame and self-punishment.

Some days, you try to wrestle control back by starving yourself. You count every calorie, each bite a measure of your worth. The hunger gnaws at you, but you tell yourself it's proof you're strong, that maybe this time you'll be good enough.

But then, the pendulum swings. The deprivation becomes unbearable, and you turn to food—not as nourishment, but as a lifeline. You binge, devouring everything in sight, trying to fill a void that food will never satisfy.

And then comes the guilt—the crushing weight of shame that sends you running to the gym or pounding the pavement. You exercise until your muscles burn, until your body screams, until you think you've punished yourself enough for the binge. And still, it doesn't feel like enough.

But your body? It's been speaking to you all along. The symptoms you're ignoring—bloating, brain fog, chronic fatigue, joint pain, restless nights, unrelenting cravings, and a weight that feels impossible to lose—are all clues. They're your body's way of saying, *Something isn't right. Pay attention.*

Here's the truth I wish you'd known then: Your body isn't your enemy. The cycle of starvation, binging, punishing workouts, and persistent symptoms isn't about willpower or failure—it's about pain and emotions that were buried deep down inside of you. And those symptoms? They aren't betrayals; they're messages.

When you begin to face the emotions you've buried—the shame, the anger, the fear—you'll realize something extraordinary. The pain starts to ease. The fog lifts. The grip food, guilt, and punishment have over your life begins to loosen.

You're not broken. You're not unlovable. You're stronger than you think you are. You're enough—exactly as you are.

Oh, the words that I wish I could tell my younger self. There is a profound connection between the chaos we endure and the control we desperately try to grasp. For years, my relationship with food mirrored my internal struggles—a pendulum swinging between deprivation and overindulgence, both of which became coping mechanisms for a life riddled with emotional, physical, and sexual trauma. This chapter is not just about my battle with an eating disorder; it is about the journey to reclaiming my body, my mind, and my power.

For most of my life, I was my own worst critic. No matter what I achieved, it never felt like enough. I pushed myself to the brink, determined to prove my worth—to myself and to others. If people needed me, if I could make them feel special, loved, and whole, maybe I could feel whole, too. This deep-rooted need to please others wasn't just kindness; it was survival. It filled the emptiness inside me and fueled my fire.

A Fragile Foundation: Mistrust and Isolation

Growing up in a small town, the very things that make me proud of who I am today—my fiery red hair and freckled complexion—became a source of relentless ridicule. What I now cherish as unique and beautiful were used as weapons against me in my formative years. The words "witch," "freak," and "ugly" were hurled at me by some of my peers, each insult chipping away at my self-worth. Even the adults, with their seemingly well-meaning comments or gestures, often crossed boundaries that left me feeling exposed and vulnerable. While I now understand that many of these interactions weren't intentionally harmful, my young mind, already conditioned by trauma, responded with instinctive panic. Every touch, every comment felt like a threat that sent me further and further into the darkness.

This reaction was not unwarranted. Within the walls of my home, a much darker reality existed. My father's words and actions shattered any semblance of safety. His physical, verbal, and sexual abuse was a constant shadow in my life, one I couldn't escape. I quickly learned that trust was a dangerous illusion. My body was not my own, my space was not sacred, and my voice was not allowed to rise above a whisper.

During my teenage years, I wasn't even allowed the small dignity of privacy. My bedroom door had no doorknob, a gut-wrenching reminder that my boundaries didn't matter. I'd catch my father staring at me through cracks in the door, his gaze stripping away what little sense of safety I had managed to build. The shame and dirtiness I felt in those moments ran so deep that it became part of my identity. I wanted nothing more than to disappear, to become invisible in my own home.

My mother, the one person I should have been able to confide in, was herself entangled in a web of abuse. My father's venomous words and physical violence left her worn and broken. Her spirit seemed to diminish under the weight of his cruelty, and I couldn't bring myself to add to her burden. I often felt like I was screaming internally, desperate for someone to hear me, but I remained silent, fearful of what might happen if I talked. She was surviving in her own way and did not have the strength to help me, even though she was a witness and sometimes a participant in the abuse.

This silence isolated me even further. The very person I yearned to turn to was unreachable, consumed by her own battles. It was as though we were both trapped in separate prisons, unable to connect through the thick walls of pain and fear that surrounded us.

To survive, I built a fortress around my emotions. I didn't let people in, because I couldn't afford to. Mistrust became my default, a reflex born out of necessity. If I couldn't trust my father, the man who was supposed to protect and love me, how could I trust anyone else? Vulnerability felt like a luxury I couldn't afford, so I armored myself with control—control over my actions, my environment, and eventually, my body.

This deep-seated mistrust didn't just shape my relationships with others; it profoundly influenced how I saw myself. I internalized the belief that I was somehow unworthy of love and protection. That self-perception laid the groundwork for the destructive behaviors that would dominate much of my young adult life. Food became both my punishment and my solace. Restricting my intake or bingeing until I was numb gave me a sense of power when everything else in my world felt uncontrollable.

The trauma of those years left a lasting imprint, but it also planted the seeds of resilience. I didn't know it then, but the pain I endured would one day fuel my determination to reclaim my sense of self, to find my voice, and to create a life where I could help others overcome their own struggles. For years, though, I shoved down the emotions and lived in survival mode, unable to see past the fortress I had built to protect myself. I would venture to say that most people who knew me never knew there was so much pain lurking in every cell of my being.

The Beginnings of Disordered Eating

Puberty added another layer of complexity. My once-skinny and underweight frame became fuller, I developed a large thyroid goiter, and the taunts only increased. I was desperate for a sense of control, something to anchor myself amidst the storm. That's when food—or the lack of it—became my refuge.

At 15, a pivotal moment occurred when my doctor, who I saw quite often, told me I needed to go on a diet. "You weigh too much. Go on a diet, and you will feel better." His words, combined with my dad's nasty insults, planted a seed that would grow into years of disordered eating. I started skipping breakfast and lunch, eating only tiny portions at dinner. Starving myself became my way of quieting the noise. Amazingly—and disturbingly—the physical effects felt like a reward. My brain fog lifted, my energy surged, and the weight melted away. For the first time, I felt a sense of accomplishment.

But with starvation came bingeing. The hunger and suppressed emotions would erupt, leading to uncontrollable eating followed by overwhelming guilt. I would then swing back to restriction, convinced that I could erase my perceived failure through further deprivation. The cycle was relentless and exhausting, but it felt like the only way to manage the chaos I couldn't control elsewhere.

Trauma's Role in the Disorder

My disordered eating wasn't just about societal pressure or body image; it was deeply rooted in trauma. The physical and sexual abuse I endured left me feeling unsafe in my own skin. Restricting food became a way to shrink myself—to become invisible, untouchable. Bingeing, on the other hand, provided temporary comfort, a way to fill the emptiness inside.

The unspoken pain of these experiences festered for years. I didn't have the tools or the support to process what had happened. So, I turned to food—and sometimes the lack of it—to manage the unmanageable.

Trapped by Escape: A Journey Through Control, Marriage, and Self-Worth

I joined the Army Reserves during my junior year of high school, desperate to escape my small town upon graduation and the suffocating home life I'd known. At the time, I was dating and became engaged to a man four years older than me, a relationship that became both an escape and a trap. He adored my small waist and thin legs, a look popularized by the "cocaine-thin" aesthetic of music videos in the late '80s and early '90s. His validation fed into my obsessive need to control my body, reinforcing the idea that my worth was tied to how I looked.

I clung to his compliments as though they were oxygen, but they came with a price. I stopped eating in public, terrified that one meal might change how he saw me or diminish the only thing I felt made me valuable. My focus wasn't on health or happiness—it was about meeting an impossible standard. I even saved my lunch money for hairspray to blend in and keep my appearance "perfect," while my body paid the price for my self-neglect. My value, I believed, was in being small, quiet, and unnoticeable—a belief born from years of being told, directly and indirectly, that I was fat, ugly, or not enough.

After graduation, my plans of leaving drastically changed the day I found out I was pregnant. It was the same day I was supposed to leave for basic training—a day that was supposed to mark the beginning of my independence and freedom. Instead, my future suddenly felt uncertain. My dreams of escape vanished, replaced with a new reality I wasn't prepared for.

I married my fiancé, convinced that we could make it work, and moved with him to Colorado, where he was transferred after joining active duty. But the life I envisioned was far from reality. My husband was uninterested in me or the baby, pouring our money into gaming, drinking, and strip clubs while I struggled to navigate motherhood alone. I was isolated, disillusioned, and emotionally abandoned. The person I had relied on to help me escape had become another source of pain. I felt invisible in my own marriage, the loneliness amplifying the emotional void I'd been trying to escape.

By my early 20s, my struggle with food had reached its peak. My weight plummeted to dangerous levels as I survived on little more than a can of tuna, cottage cheese, and pineapple or nothing at all. My skeletal frame, brittle nails, irregular periods, anxiety, and constant fatigue were cries for help my body could no longer suppress. Yet, when I looked in the mirror, all I could see was someone who was overweight and wasn't good enough. I desperately wanted to feel wanted by my husband and added laxatives to my daily routine to help keep my belly flat.

It was a vicious cycle: the less I ate, the more in control I felt, but that fleeting sense of power only deepened the emptiness inside. I'd mastered the art of masking my pain, convincing myself that control over my body could somehow fix the chaos in my heart and mind. But no amount of restriction could silence the storm of self-doubt, shame, and unresolved trauma within me.

I continued to pour everything I had into my marriage, even as it became clear that it was a one-sided effort. I believed it was my responsibility to make my husband happy—to cook, clean, and meet his every need—because that's what I had seen growing up. My mother's life revolved around keeping my father content, no matter the toll it took on her, and I had internalized the idea that this was the role of a "good wife." Divorce wasn't an option in my family; it carried too much stigma. So, I soldiered on, trying to convince myself that if I just worked harder, things would improve.

But deep down, I wanted more. I wasn't willing to let my life be defined by a rocky marriage and unfulfilled dreams. I wanted to be a good mother and still pursue a successful career—something that would prove, not only to my family but to myself, that I was capable and worthy.

Balancing Dreams and Motherhood

Determined to achieve my goals, I enrolled in night classes to pursue a nursing degree. I spent my days with my son and my nights studying, fueled by the belief that I had to excel. A 4.0 GPA and being at the top of my class weren't just goals—they were non-negotiables. I wanted to prove to my family, and perhaps to my husband, that I wasn't just "good enough." I wanted to show them that I was *somebody*.

Despite my intense focus on academics, our marriage remained strained. But we did what married people do and decided to plan for a second child to coincide with my graduation, so I could stay home with the baby for a while before launching my career. This decision brought new challenges, but it also forced me to confront one of my biggest fears: food.

Eating for the Baby

I knew that I needed to eat to nourish my baby, and for the first time since my last pregnancy, I allowed myself to eat without restriction. I promised myself I would do whatever it took to keep my baby healthy—even if it meant eating foods I had long considered off-limits. Glazed donuts became my go-to, and there were days I'd eat four to six of them in one sitting. For the first time, I felt a sense of freedom around food, but it was freedom with an asterisk.

When my second baby was born, I committed to continuing this new pattern of eating to support breastfeeding. He refused to take a bottle, so I knew his nourishment depended entirely on me. I pushed through my lingering fears about food, determined to give him everything he needed.

The Scale and the Spiral

Then came my six-week postpartum checkup. When I stepped on the scale and saw 138 pounds, panic set in. The number triggered an avalanche of old thoughts and habits. I felt like I was losing control of my body, and my eating disorder came roaring back with a vengeance.

I returned to counting every calorie, meticulously tracking everything I ate. But the restriction only fueled my urges to binge. I'd bake homemade cinnamon rolls or an entire cake, telling myself I'd have just one slice, only to devour the entire thing. The guilt would hit immediately, sending me to the gym at 3:00 in the morning to punish myself by burning off the calories.

This cycle—binge, over-exercise, restrict—became my new normal. I couldn't escape it. The harder I tried to regain control, the more out of control I felt. The bingeing filled the emptiness for a brief moment, but the shame and guilt that followed felt unbearable.

The Breaking Point: A Cycle of Control and Disconnection

The cycle of bingeing, restricting, and feeling "not enough" continued for many years, spilling into every aspect of my life. No matter how hard I tried to make my husband happy, it was never enough. I did everything I could think of—tattoos, breast implants, going to strip clubs with him, anything to hold his attention—but nothing worked. Gaming always won over me. His disinterest and emotional distance only deepened my insecurities, and I felt like I was disappearing, bit by bit, trying to mold myself into someone who might finally be "good enough."

My first job as a nurse added another layer of stress and anxiety to my already fragile world. I worked for a female doctor who, like me, was trapped in a toxic relationship. Her husband, also a doctor, frequently stormed into the office in fits of rage—throwing things, berating staff, and firing employees on the spot. The tension was palpable, and every time he entered the building, I felt like I was back in my parents' house, walking on eggshells, waiting for the next explosion.

To cope, I turned to food. Lunchtime became my escape, but it also became the stage for daily binges. I would eat until I felt numb, trying to quiet the echoes of fear and shame that lingered long after the office door slammed shut. But the temporary comfort of binging came at a cost. The restrictive behavior that followed pushed my body into rebellion. Bloating left me looking six months pregnant for days. Fatigue consumed me, and I could no longer ignore the brain fog, constipation, heavy periods, and the sense that my body was turning against me again.

The Move That Changed Everything

Our family transferred to Fort Hood, Texas, and what little connection remained in my marriage unraveled completely. My husband became more distant, consumed by gaming, while I struggled to hold our family together. His comments about my body became more cruel and controlling. He asked me not to eat, warning me that my bloating would embarrass him in public.

The breaking point came after my hysterectomy (which is a story for another time), at just 25 years old. Recovering from such a major surgery was hard enough, but his behavior made it unbearable. At a military ball just two months after my operation, I reached for bread at the dinner table. He leaned in and whispered, "Put the bread down." "Do you really think you should eat?" "You'll embarrass me if you get bloated in that dress."

Something snapped at that moment. I realized that no matter how much of myself I sacrificed, no matter how small I tried to make myself—physically or emotionally—it would never be enough for him. And, more importantly, I realized I didn't want it to be.

One month later, I made the hardest and most liberating decision of my life: I packed up and left. It wasn't just for me; it was for my boys. They deserved a mother who was strong, present, and free from the toxic cycle I had been trapped in for so long. It was time to reclaim my life, my health, and my future.

From Survival to Healing: Confronting the Root Causes of Disordered Eating

Leaving my marriage was a bold step, but it wasn't the solution to my struggles with food. What I've learned over the years is this: You can leave a toxic situation, but if you don't confront the deep-rooted emotions and beliefs causing the problem, you carry the same pain with you. I left my marriage behind, but the eating disorder came with me, just as it did when I left my parent's house, clinging to the unresolved trauma and shame I hadn't yet faced.

A New Chapter with Old Patterns

Stepping into the dating scene for the first time in my life brought excitement and attention I had never experienced before. Men called me beautiful, praised my body, and showered me with compliments. I was taken aback but also exhilarated. For the first time, I started eating more normally, even on dates.

One man, in particular, stood out. Funny, witty, and larger than life, he was also incredibly kind, intelligent, and handsome. He encouraged me to let go of my rigid food rules and try new things. I remember him convincing me to eat nachos for the first time, and to my surprise, I loved them. It felt freeing to eat without restriction, but I wasn't prepared for what would come next.

The doctor's office where I worked was overflowing with food brought in by drug reps—donuts, sandwiches, and sweets were everywhere. The X-ray room, which doubled as a breakroom, became a source of temptation. Every time I took a patient to X-ray, I would sneak snacks into my scrub pockets and eat them when I was developing the film, convincing myself I'd only eat one donut, but that quickly turned into two, three, or four.

I was allowing myself to eat freely, but my body didn't know how to handle it. Years of restriction and binging had left my digestion in chaos. My weight shot up to over 140 pounds in just a few months, and my autoimmune symptoms came roaring back. Exhaustion, bloating, brain fog, and anxiety consumed me, leaving me feeling out of control and miserable. If I was already bloated after a binge, I would tell myself, *If I am already miserable, I might as well enjoy it for a few minutes,* and keep eating.

Battling Myself

The man I was dating at the time, now my husband of over 22 years, never pressured me to look a certain way. He loved me unconditionally, filling me with compliments and connection. Yet, inside, I was relentlessly beating myself up. The pressure to be "enough" came entirely from within.

This internal war led to new levels of disordered behavior. I would chew entire pies but spit them into a bag before swallowing it, then throw them away. I'd binge on sugar-free jello, trying to fill the emotional void while avoiding the perceived damage. For a while, I was able to lose weight again by making a bet with a coworker that I could drop 20 pounds faster than she could. My competitive nature won out and I was noticed and praised for the accomplishment.

The binging and restrictive behavior continued for years, hidden behind excuses and meticulous planning. I would skip meals on Friday and all day Saturday to "earn" my nights out with my husband and friends. I convinced myself that I had control, but in reality, the eating disorder was still controlling me.

The Path to Healing

While pursuing nutrition classes and working full-time, I stumbled across a book about adrenal fatigue. I was on the stair climber for my second 90-

minute workout of the day when I thought, *Wow, this sounds like a problem... but not for me.* Looking back, it's clear that I was deep in denial.

Transitioning my career into holistic nutrition was the turning point I desperately needed. It wasn't just about learning to heal my body—it was about learning to heal myself. I reversed my autoimmune symptoms, and I began to gain control over what I put into my body. More importantly, I started to address the emotional wounds that had driven my eating disorder for so long.

At 33 years old, I wrote a letter to my parents. I poured out the pain and anger I had carried for years, telling them how deeply their actions had hurt me and how wrong their behavior was. I don't know if they ever read the letter, but sending it was transformative. It broke the bond of trauma that had held me captive for so long. I felt a sense of freedom I hadn't known before, a release that allowed me to begin truly loving myself.

By 35, I felt physically amazing. My autoimmunity was under control, and I was thriving in my new career as a holistic nutritionist. By 38, the binging and restrictive behaviors had mostly faded. But every now and then, during times of stress or when life felt out of control, I would still find myself slipping back into old patterns.

Doing the Deep Work

It wasn't until I was 47 that I was ready—or perhaps forced—to confront the deepest layers of my pain. Life has a way of presenting us with opportunities to heal when we least expect them. For me, this meant diving into the deep-rooted limiting beliefs and unresolved emotions that had been lurking beneath the surface for decades.

Through mindset work, energy healing, and Neuro-Linguistic Programming (NLP), I uncovered and released the stories I had been telling myself for years: that I wasn't good enough, that I had to be perfect to be loved, that my worth was tied to how small or "in control" I could make myself.

This work was not easy, but it was necessary. It allowed me to step fully into my power and create a life of purpose and fulfillment. Today, I use these same tools to guide my clients through their own journeys of healing.

A Safe Space for Women to Heal

Looking back, I can see that my obsession with perfection fueled this cycle as much as my unresolved trauma. I believed that if I could just have the perfect body, be the perfect mom, and excel in my career, I could prove my worth—not just to my family, but to myself. I thought that achieving these external markers of success would silence the voice in my head that constantly told me I wasn't good enough.

But the truth was, I wasn't addressing the root of the problem. My eating disorder wasn't about food or weight; it was about control. It was my way of managing the pain and chaos that had followed me from childhood.

My journey has taught me that healing is not linear and that true transformation requires more than surface-level solutions. I created my practice to provide women with a safe space to uncover and address the root causes of their struggles—whether it's disordered eating, unresolved trauma, or the weight of limiting beliefs.

I help women reconnect with their bodies, rebuild trust in themselves, and create lives where they feel strong, confident, and empowered. Healing isn't about perfection; it's about progress, and it starts with giving yourself permission to let go of what no longer serves you.

If you've ever felt stuck in cycles of self-doubt, shame, or physical symptoms you can't seem to shake, know this: You are not alone. Healing is possible, and you are worthy of a life filled with freedom, joy, and self-love. Let's take this journey together.

Ariel Balfour

Trauma 2 Triumph Coaching Inc.
Emotional Wellness Mentor, Owner & CEO

https://www.facebook.com/ariel.sommers/
https://www.instagram.com/thearielbalfour
https://www.thearielbalfour.com/

Ariel Balfour, known as the Viking Queen and Reclamation Warrior, is a force in emotional wellness, transforming how we approach mental health and trauma. With a warrior's heart forged in MMA and a soul deeply connected to collective consciousness, Ariel blends ancient wisdom with modern techniques to help others reclaim their power and their truth. Her raw, edgy approach shatters traditional norms, guiding people through their darkest battles to emerge stronger and more empowered. Unapologetic in her mission, Ariel is a fierce advocate for emotional resilience, showing that true strength lies in embracing vulnerability and facing the chaos head-on. Her journey is one of deep spiritual connection, strength, and transformation, offering a path for others to reclaim their calm, their power, and their life. She's not a therapist—she's the warrior leading a revolution in healing.

Silent Rage Can Be Deafening

By Ariel Balfour

The corners of my vision go red as I will myself to leave my body before the sensation of complete betrayal hits like a crashing wave.

Anger was not a new emotion to me, nor was completely losing control to it. In fact, it felt like a blanket of comfort and power. It felt like home. Anger had always been an internal story I lived with and played with but *never* showed until it erupted in a catastrophic event. I learned the lessons about letting the anger out and the devastation it left behind. From the moment I came into this world to this very moment, I came filled with a force I had no idea how to harness. I fell into it.

Another wave of blinding pain hits as I try to focus on the mass amounts of doctors and student nurses that surround me. I can't hear their voices, but I know what is being said. All choices are gone. My body is no longer my own temple but theirs. Bound and broken with no hope left. The rage follows behind the pain like a gentle whisper of comfort, **Let them hear you, hurt them like they hurt you.**

10, 9, 8, 7, 6, 5, 4, 3, 2, 1. Breathe. I shake my head, pushing the rage aside as the pain dissipates for this very brief moment. Sweat dripped in my eyes as I glared at the team before me. Each one taking their turn inside my sacred temple, not to help but to learn—a cold and untrusting practice. Blank, compassionless faces observing me, prodding me like a caged animal for their interests and pleasure. Twisted scientists, hungry for the results they so desire.

"Ariel, I am willing to give you 30 more minutes before we call this, but I think you are done. It is late, and you are not pushing this baby into the canal. I believe it is time we call the surgeon," the doctor tells me with self-serving pity in her eyes. As the realization of losing my first battle ever comes crashing down on me, the next contraction takes my breath away with it.

As I blindly fall back into pain, the rage darkens everything, I am unable to see or hear anything. I reflect back at this moment on everything that led me to my ultimate failure as a fighter. This was never meant to unfold this way, I was a champion, and I never lost. Until now. A battle I was ill-prepared for.

My brain floats back to 3 days prior, already 10 days late and 2 sweeps later, to try and stick to the harsh timeline set before us from the medical world. It was 5 a.m. when my husband shot up out of bed after another back spasm woke us for a third and final time.

"I'll head to the couch; you need to get your sleep," he says groggily.

"Would you like a blanket?" I ask concerned. He turns to nod as he stumbles down the hallway, still half asleep. I throw my fully pregnant belly off the side of the bed, allowing the momentum to pull the rest of my body with it. This was the only way to get out of bed these days and it was amusing, to say the least. I smile to myself knowing this might be the last day I do such a silly move.

As I waddle to the spare room and grab the blanket, a guttural raw scream pierces the air like a tortured animal caught in a steel trap. Everything tenses in my body as I demand my oversized body to move fast towards the screams against my all-natural instinct to run away. The screams grow more intense as I enter the living room, seeing my husband rolling around on the ground as if possessed.

I try to take in the scene before me as quickly as possible to determine the next steps. I gaze at his bare back, shocked as I stare in disbelief, seeing the muscles moving like snakes within his back. It was straight out of every horror movie I had ever watched, how could this be real life?

Curling, coiling, attacking from within, his body is not his own. His screams are deafening as I somehow find the strength to run for my phone to dial 911 and call my team at the Ambulance hall, as I know this would mean all hands on deck... I also know the baby is coming, and the time is now.

As my teams arrive to cart my husband away, I hop into my jeep, squeezing into the seat as the first waves of contractions start. ***Not now, baby, come on, we have work to do first. We got to help Daddy!*** I race off at unimaginable speeds towards the hospital, chasing the ambulance, desperate to be by his side.

I enter the hospital and am greeted with another guttural cry, responding in kind. Walking into the room, I watch as my husband physically tries to crawl away from his own body as if he could free himself from his tortured cage. I go to his bedside as my crew is working diligently to catch the nurses up to speed and look into the eyes of a grown man, but all I can see is a scared little boy searching for any relief. As he begins to spasm again, his eyes rolling back, every muscle contorting to fight the pain, as if in sync, the contraction takes hold of my body, a beautifully tortured dance.

"Ummm, are you ok?" my teammate says aloud.

Breathing heavily my husband squeaks out, "Yes, it was just another spasm."

"Not you...her!" she nervously points towards me as I grip the bar on the bed, trying to steady my breath and remain in control. As our eyes meet, I see the panic, the realization hitting him harder than the spasms rocking his body.

10, 9, 8, 7, 6, 5, 4, 3, 2, 1. Breathe.

I am snapped back into the room as another faceless nurse takes their turn inside my body to assess me. The violation of my space and inner wisdom begins to build towards an eruption of pure unhinged rage. Still no success. ***Yea, no shit, stay the fuck out of my body and let me be. I am not here for your sick pleasure.***

The next contraction comes in unforgiving before I even have a chance to breathe fully. I am lost again to the void within, reliving where the mistakes were made, which in truth, only serves the ravenous rage within.

After realizing that the contractions were too close together with our northern hospital unequipped for delivery, I was faced with the very daunting task of getting myself to another facility 45 minutes away. I had already enlisted my brother in a complete panic, knowing beyond a doubt he would move heaven and earth to get to me, but that was still a 12-hour drive, so I had begun to create other plans. I begged for the help of a local, very ill-prepared doula to get me to my destination. As I sit bouncing on a ball waiting to be assessed, I roll with the natural waves of contractions, breathing, fighting off the never-ending worry that my husband may very well miss the birth of his first child.

As this thought fades, I see him stumble into my room, a friend by his side, like always, my knight in shining armour just battered and bruised from the fields of war.

"You made it!!" I exclaim with excitement and worry, "Take my bed and rest. I don't need it right now."

"Thanks, are you sure?" he asks gratefully. I nod, certain that I want him in the best shape possible for what's to come.

As I close my eyes with the next contraction, I am ripped from it with the all-too-familiar piercing scream. He begins to claw his way up the bed, willing himself to leave his own body yet again and the onslaught of torture being bestowed upon him. The nurse comes in quickly, her shock clearly defined, as her eyes dart from me to my husband.

"What's going on here?" her voice quivering with false confidence.

"His back is spasming and needs a doctor! It just went out this morning." I yell back, concern for his well-being becoming my number one priority. "Take him to emergency NOW! They should never have released him."

"Can you walk?" she tried to yell over his scream. My rage boils dangerously close to the surface as her ignorance slashes at my thin cords of patience.

"Obviously not, take my bed, he needs help!" The demanding leadership dripping in ever word. No was not an option she could take. She rushes over to take him away as I roll on the ball listening to his screams fading but never gone. The rage threatens to release, so I let the tears fall instead, knowing tears are safer for everyone.

10, 9, 8, 7, 6, 5, 4, 3, 2, 1. Breathe.

Back in my body, feeling defeated as the words *"Baby still hasn't moved"* hit me like a brick wall. All the information is now being directed at my husband, who is holding on by a drug-induced thread, determined to be there for me, but even he knows this decision is mine alone. His eyes search mine, desperate for the answer.

The tears spill, and the volcano erupts "Fuck all of you, you did this, you KNEW this is how it was going to end!! You wanted this! Fine, fuck you all, I failed, I give up!! YOU FUCKING WIN!" I collapse back into bed, feeling grief rack my body. The one thing I was built to do, the one battle I was destined to beat, and I failed. Utterly and completely. The grief suffocated me as rage buried me alive. I choose to leave my body again, broken and defeated.

As I float back to torture myself with every moment where this defeat is set in motion, the realization that the champion had died within me was more than I can bear, but I deserve this torture as my penance.

Three days of active labouring, being turned away because I didn't meet requirements but never being sure if I would make it to the hospital in time, three days of absolute hell. The stress builds and becomes unbearable as the doctor set a timeline on my body. A timeline meant for doctors not natural progression. My brother, as predicted, arrived ready to aid in any way he could, which meant not just me but my husband as well, who was now laid up on the floor in insurmountable pain.

Everyone looking at me with pity only fed my internal rage. This was not meant to happen like this. My husband wasn't meant to be hurt, I wasn't supposed to meet a timeline set by someone else, none of it. I already had my desire for a home birth ripped from me due to northern regulations, which was only the start of my rights being stripped from me.

At 3 a.m. on the third and final day, only hours before the deadline, I knew it was time. As we rushed off to the hospital, knowing that either way, this time, I could not be turned away, my thoughts went back to my husband, willing him to make it and not have another attack.

The next 24 hours blurred and raced by in shattered time, each tragic moment building on the next. The doula I came to know, love, and trust was unable to attend till almost the end of the 3 days. Doctors and nurses, I did not agree to when of sound mind, thrust upon me like a prospect within a brothel, faces, and energy unknown to me. The violation of my sacred right to say no, and coercion became the toxic trait of the day. Fear-mongering was the drink to wash it all down with.

The moments of violation flooding my system as a constant reminder that my body is not my own, bringing the rage I felt from past experiences exploding to the surface, my mind begging to disconnect to end the reminder. My body has not been my own before, with no control over what happens next, resigning to the truth that I am merely here for others to do as they please. The rage became more potent, drowning me in crimson red.

10, 9, 8, 7, 6, 5, 4, 3, 2, 1. Breathe.

"Hi Ariel, I am Dr. Ho, I am here for the epidural for your c-section." He says professionally. We lock eyes as sympathy and compassion flood his face. "I'm sorry this is how it has happened till now but do not worry, I am here and will ensure everything goes smoothly on my end."

With his silky-smooth brown eyes locked on mine, for the first time in nearly 72 hours, I leaned into trust, his trust, knowing somehow his compassion was true. His work from that moment on was meticulous and quick but never wavering in care. Before I could even blink, the pain subsided, my eyes glazing over as I followed the line from the wall to the ceiling, being guided down by strange hands. Resignation settling in as fast as the numbing agent flooding my system.

The tears of failure burst out against my will, grief racking my body once more. Listening but not truly hearing all of the voices around me as they try to soothe me, using fake empathy to validate this defeat. I knew in that moment the war had been lost and I had been so focused on the battle I didn't see the mercenaries sneak in and silently end it before my eyes.

As a woman, I felt that I failed completely but was told at least the baby was healthy, and we both survived, but not one person could look me in the eyes without shame. I knew. I knew what had truly conspired, and in that moment, the rage bubbled and boiled beneath the surface, threatening to emerge.

5, 4, 3, 2, 1. Breathe. The cries of my firstborn drown out all other thoughts and sounds at that moment. All else fell away.

Seven days is what it took for that rage to finally erupt. Seven days to release but not fully, release in a way not even I saw coming. When things didn't seem like they could get worse, the universe reminded me once again that emotions repressed become expressed, whether you like it or not. That day, day seven, my life changed forever.

As my eyes groggily open, hearing the sweet coos and shifts of my new babe beside me, I feel a sense of contentment with a dash of exhaustion. Gingerly, I begin to roll and sit up, being mindful of the cut that crossed my belly like a constant reminder of the battle I had lost, though I was assured it was a scar of honor. *Pfffft, yea, said everyone who ever lied.* As I gently grab my baby boy, in awe of his perfection, I feel an odd tingle in the side of my face, like the sensation of a sleeping limb waking in its first moments. I rub my face vigorously as I adjust my son to feed him.

Being in the throes of first love can be blindingly beautiful, but something keeps gnawing at me, a feeling I just can't shake. As he suckles gently, I begin to take stock of this surmounting feeling of dread and impending doom. *Come on, Ariel, get it together; you are just sleep-deprived and still mentally healing from this experience.* I notice in that moment my eye feels puffy and watery, wiping away the liquid, and the fear creeps back in. *What is happening?* The pit in my stomach begins to grow.

As I put my son back in the bassinet, the feeling only builds as I decide to go get ready for the day, willing the sensation to go away. I carefully walk myself down the hall to the bathroom and shut the door as my heart begins to pound. My eyes lifted to meet my own gaze but instead met the distorted gaze of a complete stranger. I stare in complete and utter disbelief. The right side of my face had completely drooped, and as a paramedic, I knew of only one reason this would happen, *stroke.* My mind begins to panic and race as the realization that as time ticks by, this may be irreversible damage or, even worse, fatal.

Breathe, Ariel, you have been on many of these calls, just FAST VAN. My brain trying to speak logic to me as I begin to run through the tests. But as soon as I begin, a voice within my head sucker punches me. *You can't test yourself, Ariel, our brain thinks it knows what is happening but won't appear that way outwardly. Fuck, fuck, fuck, this is bad, like really, really bad!* I take a deep breath, allowing my brain the moment of reprieve as I disconnect and fool myself into waiting it out because this is just a weird reaction to meds. *Ahhhh, the logic of self-diagnosing paramedic determined to avoid our health system, kudos to you, Ariel.* I sniff as I straighten to wash my face, moving on like a bad high school date, forgotten before it even began.

I go to grab my son and join the family visiting in the living room, ensuring I turn my head to take the focus from my mangled face. Carrying on as if everything is normal, fooling almost everyone until my husband walks in the room, with a concerned look developing.

"Ariel, are you ok, you sound funny," he says with deep care.

"Ya, I'm good, just tired," I quickly respond as I turn my head.

"Look at me." He now says with a commanding voice. I turn my face to meet his gaze as horror crosses his face, the deep pit in my stomach twisting and turning in response. "What the hell! Did you have a stroke?"

"No, I don't know, doubt it! I did a fast van, it's fine. I don't want to go back to the hospital. What if they keep me, I have a baby to care for. It's fine." I speak quickly, my voice wavering with fear.

"Ariel, I think you had a stroke. You need to go and go now. What would you tell a patient if you were on scene, and they said this to you?" he asks with determination.

I lower my eyes as the tears leak out slowly with the realization, he was right. "I would tell them they didn't have a choice and needed to go."

We pack up swiftly as I kiss my baby goodbye, the fear of not knowing when I would see him next settling in like a dark cloud, rage at the ready. The ride to the hospital was a silent and somber one, fear enveloping all of our thoughts. Luckily, the ride is only five minutes away, and we enter the hospital and take a seat in the emergency room, being ushered through the check-in process swiftly and efficiently.

I sit cradling my face, willing myself to awake from the nightmare I was sure to be in, but time kept on with no relief. Just then, a coworker clearly packing up from a current emergent call comes around the corner, a smile on his face as he sees me.

"Hey, Ariel, what are you doing here? Justin, did your back go again?" he asks happy to see us but concern evident in his tone.

I look up with shame, knowing I would have to see that look of horror yet again. "No, I think I had a stroke."

His eyes widen with concern, but he quickly moves into paramedic neutrality and compassion, "Ok, let me go talk with the nurses. Don't worry, we got you." He quickly vacates my side to go talk with the nurse in charge, sure to see me in, as quickly as possible.

Everything seems to swirl by in an instance, being hooked up to many electrodes, many nurses moving with ease in a dance of momentum. The doctor enters the room, and everything snaps back into clear focus.

"Well, didn't expect to see you guys here again so soon, but I come bearing great news. You did NOT have a stroke!" he exclaims with a smile from ear to ear. "However, I believe you have experienced a phenomenon called 'Bells Palsy.' There is no real evidence as to why it happens or treatments, but we have had great success using antivirals and steroids. This will be gone in a matter of days or a week."

Relief relaxes every muscle in my body but not my frozen face. I practice a moment of gratitude. *I was not majorly injured, and this is reversible*, I tell myself. "Will it all go back to normal, my face, I mean? This is awful, I look awful." I say outwardly defeated.

"We don't know exactly how long this will take, but yes, you will heal. Be glad it wasn't a stroke." His tone changes from excitement to annoyance. "It's just a face, no need to focus on what doesn't matter."

But to me, it did. The rage that was still simmering beneath the surface builds once more, my face contorting to match. "Well, it does since I coach online as well," I state angrily. "Ok, so what happens now?"

Mindful Her | 85

"Well, you need to take the antiviral, but that means no breastfeeding. As well—" My head snaps around as he states this.

"ABSOLUTELY NOT! This is the one thing, the one fucking thing that has gone my way in the entirely fucked-up situation! No! What else can we do?"

He sighs, annoyance turning to anger, "Well, you can just do the steroids but it's just breastfeeding, and if you want to fix this, you should try everything and just get over it. Baby will be fine."

"NO," I state with absolution. "What is the success rate even if I did?"

"We don't know. These are just the suggestions, trials even, but no, we don't know if any of it actually works as there has not been enough research." He glances at his watch.

"Ok, I will try the steroids, but risking the one thing working for us for a maybe does not work for me." The rage begins to simmer as I take my power back. The doctor lets out a big sigh and nods as he goes to write the prescription.

I thought reclaiming my no would make it better, but I sat day in and day out in front of the mirror, wondering if I had made the right decision. The rage of yet another blow to my ego hitting harder and deeper than before. I am now a stranger to myself. Staring at the lopsided smile frozen in grief. The eye, wide with terror, unable to close. This person in the mirror was unknown to me, a weak and broken version of what once was a powerhouse.

The days promised for healing quickly turned to weeks with no change, and the rage bubbled and brimmed higher and more potent by the day. My mental health took a beating as shame swirled like a tornado with devastating results, but the words that always left my mouth were, "I'm fine." **Sure, freaked out, insecure, neurotic, and emotional, yep, you are F.I.N.E.**

Weeks turned into seasons flying by as treatment after treatment was explored, the stranger in the mirror changing more into a shell of a human. The voices of everyone around stated the obvious without truly understanding the impact of their words. "At least the baby is healthy," "It's just a face, what matters most is your heart," "You got the baby; everyone will be focused on him anyways." With each attempt at soothing the darkness that surrounded me, all I wanted to do was scream and lash out, causing physical damage to their face, so they might have even a moment of understanding. But I continued to swallow the rock of hatred down further until it grew like a weight in my stomach to match the pounds I packed on to hide away beneath.

Six months of this led me straight to my wedding day, a day full of magic and love, and yet all I felt was rage and resentment. Every camera click reminded me of the horror that would be reflected in the picture they took. The rage now blinded me so much that everything blurred into one numbed-out night. Little did I know that beneath this rage was the ultimate emotion I chose to ignore...sadness, but I wasn't ready to face that yet.

Seasons grew into years without any change. I was numb to it all. People's comments changed to things like "I barely notice anymore" "Hey, it's looking better, it will be healed in no time," or my personal level of hell, "Hey, it could be worse." ***Thanks for the ignorant support.*** The silent rage now seeping out like poison all around me, I began to lose friends, strain my relationship, and feel resentment in every moment. Happiness felt like it was not an option; grief and rage were all I knew in that moment.

Looking in the mirror as I did every day, hating what I saw, this time shattering, I knew I needed help. In that moment, a choice had to be made. Die from the self-inflicted poison of rage that coursed through my veins or deep dive into the realms of self-actualization and healing, a walk through beautiful pain. As I stared at my contorted face, I caught a glimpse for the first time in over a year of the warrior within. My inner warrior had not abandoned me, she was ready to do the work and was waiting for me to see it.

Healing is a journey and not a destination. This has been my mantra for the last five years; a reminder that progress over perfection is a true gift. As I journeyed through the realms within, healing my inner child, raging with the inner teenager, and comforting the scared adult, I got to see myself in the light and in the ways that others saw me. Realizing that my scars were only known to me and it was I who created the rage within. But it was also me who needed to be the saviour and choose a different path.

Tonya Rachelle Rebhahn

CEO of Chain Breakers Mindset Coaching

https://www.facebook.com/1AvaJames
https://www.instagram.com/chainbreakers_mindset_coaching/
https://www.chainbreakersmindsetcoaching.com/

Tonya is a transformational holistic coach who focuses on the mind, body, spirit connection. She is certified in NLP, Hypnotherapy and Holistic Nutrition. People hire her to find the missing piece of why they can't overcome chronic weight gain or pain and illness because they are sick and tired of feeling sick and tired. She helps them overcome previous trauma, reduce stress, and achieve whole body wellness.

Divine Protection

By Tonya Rachelle Rebhahn

It's hard to know where to begin one's story properly. It's even harder to know exactly where one starts to begin their mental decline. According to the Adverse Childhood Experiences Study, or ACE Study, conducted by the CDC and Kaiser Permanente, Big T and Little t traumas in childhood can contribute to mental and physical issues later in life. Trauma is "Any event beyond the person's ability to master at the time." Some examples of Big T traumas are war, natural disasters, domestic violence, rape, domestic abuse, child abuse, and bullying. Some examples of little t trauma could be: divorce, yelling, family secrets, the death of a loved one, and moving, but everyone reacts differently to events. Keeping these things in mind, I find it only appropriate to begin here.

I remember sitting on my parents' bed in their bedroom. I believe I was six years old. My mom and dad were looking down at me, and my father told me that they had decided that they were going to be getting a divorce. I wasn't sure if I should be upset by that, because they were constantly fighting. And I don't just mean yelling, either. I didn't know what a "divorce" would look like, but I remember thinking it might be safer for both of them.

This divorce ended up meaning me living with my grandma mostly for a while while my dad worked all the time in the city, and my mom did a lot of hard partying. She was too busy meeting new men to have time for me. This led to more fighting between my parents, even though they were not together anymore.

Eventually, my dad decided he wanted to move away from the city. He had a hunting shack up in Wisconsin and decided we were going to move into it and make it into a home. I started a new school there, and on the first day of school, I was labeled "cootie girl" and got the air knocked out of me by a boy on the playground at lunchtime.

I wish I could say that this was just a first-day-of-school event; however, I remained "the cootie girl." I was picked on and treated horribly by my classmates until the day I graduated high school. I eventually upgraded from being the "cootie girl" to instead becoming a " cow and moose" in later grades when I became a bit chunky. They would moo at me when I walked by. I also got tormented for being poor and having a crappy car, a crappy house, and ugly clothes.

Also, my mother decided to move in with my father to our house in Wisconsin. This was a very bad thing. Things would get very violent and chaotic. They were on again and off again with their relationship. Eventually, she left him for a man and got pregnant. This was when I was 10 years old. My mom married the man right before she was due to have her baby. My dad started dating a new woman at this time as well.

One night, I was sitting on the couch at home with my dad, and the phone rang. It was my stepdad. He called to let me know my mom had the baby and asked to speak to my father. When my dad hung up the phone, he told me he was taking me to Rochester, Minnesota, to see my mom because she was not doing well.

When I got to my mother's hospital room, my aunts and stepdad explained to me that after my mom had the baby, she ended up having a brain aneurysm. She was only being kept alive by machines, but they wanted me to be able to say goodbye. At that moment, all I could think about was how the last time I saw her and the last thing I told her was I hated her.

Outside, it was storming hard. It was just like the type of setting you would expect in a movie when something tragic happens. I went to the side of the bed and said, "Goodbye." I didn't know what else to do or say. My aunts asked me if I wanted them to take me downstairs. I shook my head yes. We walked up to the elevators, and as we went to push the button, all of a sudden, the doors started to open and shut quickly back and forth in front of us. I still wonder if that was the storm or something more.

Is it hard losing your mother at ten? Yes, but I'm not sure if it would have been harder if I had had a close relationship with her, or if it's harder feeling like you had a mom who didn't care much about you and that the last words you told her were hateful ones.

My father came from a broken home as well; he was the oldest of four siblings, and his father abandoned them and my grandma when my dad was only nine. My grandma had done all she could do to feed them, and my dad was out on his own at only 15. He had a hard life, and it made him hard. He did the best he could to raise me, but it was not a very loving, compassionate home. It was a tough-love home because that is all he knows. Crying or showing "feelings" was a sign of weakness. And mental weakness was not okay in my family. It was unacceptable. I don't know how many times I heard "toughen up, buttercup."

I learned to turn hurt into anger. It seemed safer as a teen to channel pain as aggression rather than tears in front of my family. I started lifting weights a lot and got into sports because I had to be "strong." I wanted to make my father proud; he was all I had, after all.

Through high school, I had severe depression. I hated being treated like an outcast in school. I wanted to be the "popular girl," just once. I wanted to feel pretty instead of fat. I wanted to have boys like me. I also didn't know what to do with my life, the last thing in the world I wanted was to be poor like my dad. I wanted to be somebody. I wanted to be respected instead of looked down upon like my family always was, but I didn't know how I could get out of the hole and afford college. My dad was discouraging me from going to college, he said it was a waste of money.

During my senior year, I ended up getting an academic scholarship for college, not a full ride but enough to help. I also made the college volleyball team. In my first semester of college, I ended up getting raped by a man who lived in my dorm, and depression ended up getting the better of me. I dropped out of school and got on the list for school closer to home to become a dental hygienist. In the meantime, I started working in a bar. Little did I know this would lead to the greatest mistake of my life.

One night while working, I met a man who I found very attractive, and he asked me out. We ended up dating. There were many red flags about this man that I ignored. When you grow up being bullied and treated as an outcast, you develop really low self-esteem and just want to be loved. This man was wishy-washy with me, and I would catch him in lies. When I first met him, I found out he was adopted, but he had reunited with his biological father. He was at the time living in his biological father's trailer house with him. He had apparently had a "falling-out" with his adoptive parents.

We were dating for a while, and during that period, he reconciled with his adoptive parents and moved back in with them, so we had a long-distance relationship. He had been making up different excuses not to see me, and I started having suspicions he was cheating, so I broke up with him. He called me one night and told me he would kill himself if I didn't come see him. So, I went to see him. I can't remember the exact conversation, but he was being manipulative, and I told him I was leaving. He took a knife out and slit his one wrist. I freaked out and got him help. Of course, then I agreed to stay with him because I was afraid he would do it again.

I ended up getting pregnant by him that same night! At the young age of 19 years old. I was terrified when I found out. When my boyfriend's mother found out, she suggested I get an abortion, but that didn't seem like an option to me. When my dad found out, he kicked me out of the house, and I moved in with my grandma.

I had been paying for a cell phone plan that my boyfriend and I both used. We were still in a long-distance relationship while he lived with his parents. He was four years older than me. One night, when I was eight months pregnant, I was going through our cell phone bill. I noticed a number on there that I didn't recognize. It was attached to my boyfriend's cell number. I decided to call it. A woman answered. I asked her how she had his number. She explained to me that they had met at a bar and had slept together. I asked her if she knew he had a pregnant girlfriend. She explained to me that he told her he was expecting a baby, but he was no longer with the mother of the baby. I explained to her that was a lie, we were just together over the weekend. I asked her if he had worn a condom when they were together. She said he didn't want to. I dropped the phone. I was shaking, I wanted to throw up. I didn't know what to do. Not only had he betrayed me, but he didn't even care about the safety of our unborn child. The pain was too much for me to bear. That, to this day, is the worst pain I have ever felt. I felt like all my dreams were shattered. I was going to be a loser single mom struggling my whole life to get by and bringing a baby into a cruddy life. I went and got a knife and ran a bath. I lay in the bath and put the knife to my wrist. Then I heard a whisper in my head, "Tonya, how dare you do that to a baby?" I put the knife down and cried for what seemed like hours.

I didn't speak or see my ex anymore until the night I went into labor. I thought it was the right thing to do to let him know. He came to the hospital. He, of course, was apologizing and saying how he wanted to make things right. Me being vulnerable and scared to be a single mom, I let him back into my life. It didn't help that I didn't have much family support, either. We ended up moving in together and getting engaged. Two weeks before we were set to get married, I received the first black eye of many to come from him.

I can't even remember when it was over. I just remember being stunned at the time and not knowing what to do about it. It was so close to the wedding. If I canceled, I would have been humiliated and lost out on lots of money. I decided to ignore it and hoped it would never happen again, but as I'm sure you guessed, that was not the case.

I endured five years of brutal abuse. We had two boys together. One night, he was out to the bars like usual, and I couldn't sleep. It was 3 a.m., so I couldn't help but wonder what kind of trouble he had gotten into or who he might be with. I then heard his pickup pull up the driveway. I looked out my bedroom window and saw the side of his truck dented up. I went outside. As he staggered out the door, I said, "What did you do?" Then, I saw the look in his eyes change. I knew that look. That was the look that meant I better get out of there. I turned around and headed back for the house, but right before I made it to the door, he took me down from behind. He got on top of me and started hitting my head against the concrete. Somehow, I broke free from him and just made it to the door of the house when he took me down again and, this time, started strangling me. My five-year-old must have heard the commotion because he came into the kitchen, and when he saw what his dad was doing, he jumped on his back to try and get him off. This made my ex stand up to get my son off of him. I ran for the phone, but he came and ripped the phone off the wall. Then somehow, by the grace of God, he ended up passing out. I knew I had to escape. I grabbed my five- and two-year-old, their blankets, and my purse. We first went to the hospital. They did a CAT scan on my head to check for internal bleeding and then measured the fingertip bruising on my neck and other areas. They said I may need that for filing a police report. They then called a woman's shelter and told them we were on our way for protection.

It was not an easy road from here, but it was a road well worth traveling. Fortunately, by the time I left him, I had put myself through dental hygiene school, even with a baby and another on the way, and had started working as a dental hygienist. I was determined to prove to myself that nothing was impossible. And part of that was stubbornness because my dad told me I would never be able to make it through school once I got pregnant, and I wanted to prove him wrong.

So, even though I left with nothing and my husband cut my finances off and was not paying any child support, the women's shelter provided us with some clothing and basic needs, and I was able to keep working my job to be able to come up with a downpayment to hire a divorce lawyer.

My ex and his family fought very dirty and tried everything they could to destroy me and take the children from me, so he would not have to pay child support. My ex left messages on my boss's phone saying lies to try and get me fired from my job, so I would not have any money coming in. He would call child protection services on me and tell them I was abusing my kids. He would also drive by my apartment non-stop to intimidate me once I got my own place. His best friend was a state trooper, and he would find out the address to wherever I moved from him so he could stalk me. Once, I hired a babysitter to go out, and he kept calling the babysitter asking where I went and scared her!

Eventually, I met a wonderful man who I started dating. He caught wind of that and went to his hometown and started asking questions about him at local businesses to try and find out who he was until he found out his cell number from someone. He then proceeded to call my new boyfriend and tell him how I was psychotic. I was still sleeping with him, and some other lies. Fortunately, my new boyfriend was smart enough to realize who the real psycho was. This wonderful man named Tad ended up marrying me even with all these problems.

After spending about $37,000 on lawyer fees and two years of court battles, my ex was over $40,000+ in debt in back child support. They finally decided to start going after him for it. He had been given initially weekend visitation of the boys and didn't use it, but then it was changed, I gave him an offer he couldn't refuse for my and the boys' best interest. I told him if he would sign off on the boys, I would sign off on all back child support, and he would never owe any going forward. He agreed, and Tad adopted the boys! I was free from the nightmare at last!

Besides, he had new problems to deal with. He had gotten remarried and had a new baby. He had put the new wife in the hospital with broken bones already. He was going to be going through another custody battle. He didn't want to be dealing with two women at the same time.

While I was going through my divorce, I lost like 30 lbs from the stress. I was thinking now that I had a new, wonderful husband and that the divorce was over, life would finally start looking up for me. So I thought...

Life was better for a few years. It was almost too good. It was too normal. I had a stable family household where my only stress was my job and co-workers. It actually was terrifying at times. When you have lived a life of constant trauma and chaos, when things are good, you are constantly waiting for the next bad thing to happen. The longer of a break you have from bad things, the bigger the fall from grace will be, you fear.

One day at work, I wasn't feeling well. I was feeling like I had the flu, and then suddenly, my body started shaking in convulsions. I went to the hospital, and a few of my lab values were off, but they were not sure what had caused the episode, so they sent me home, figuring it was a virus. The problem was I continued to have problems. I had tremors that were more pronounced in my right hand, which just happened to be my dominant hand. This is a very bad thing if your job requires you to go into people's mouths with sharp instruments. For some reason, people get a little concerned when they see a sharp blade coming at them in a shaky hand. But that wasn't all. I was severely fatigued. I had digestive issues with nausea and dizzy spells. I was getting on-and-off rashes, migraines, and joint pain. I would go through on/off bouts of throwing up and would occasionally pass out. Also, I had more episodes where my entire body would get convulsive.

I went to Dr. Google. At first, I was thinking I had multiple sclerosis. I had all the symptoms, plus more. I ended up getting into neurology for an evaluation after my general doctor ruled out some other potential causes. The neurologist came in after the MRI and said she did not see any sign of M.S., but there was some optic nerve prominence and flattening of the pituitary gland that could indicate excessive spinal fluid. They would have to do some further testing on that with a spinal tap. She went on to ask me some more questions. One of the questions she asked me was if I had ever experienced any type of head injury. To that, I explained the night that my ex had hit my head against our concrete patio. I saw the look on her face change. She then went on to tell me how there is a strong mind-body connection and things like PTSD could manifest physically in a body. I explained to her that it had been years since the abuse, and it wasn't until recently that my symptoms showed up. She didn't seem to think that mattered. She referred me to a psychiatrist for PTSD evaluation and counseling.

I did see the psychologist, but I strongly felt that there was more to it than just PTSD causing my physical manifestations, so I started doing a lot of research on my own about health and neuroscience. After getting what felt like a lot of gaslighting from my doctors, I found out about a rare disease specialist out of Atlanta, Georgia, who had a good reputation in figuring out situations like mine. She didn't take insurance because she did not like how insurance would dictate the level of care her clients got. She did a bunch of tests, including genetic testing. By the end, I ended up finding out I had multiple things going against me. I received a diagnosis of Lyme disease with co-infections, a rare disease called Ehlers-Danlos syndrome, and later Lupus as well.

At first, I was angry with my doctors. SAY, I told you so. I knew there was something physically wrong with me, but the more I researched, I learned they were probably not 100% wrong about the diagnosis being trauma-related. So, let me explain to you why and how this could be impacting you.

Earlier, I mentioned The Adverse Childhood Experiences (ACE) Study. This study found a strong correlation between early childhood trauma and a higher risk of developing various chronic diseases in adulthood. The more adverse childhood experiences you have, the higher your risk. The idea that childhood trauma could create a propensity toward illness later in life is based on several interconnected mechanisms involving the body's stress response, immune function, and psychological health. Key factors include: chronic stress response, immune system dysregulation, behavioral factors, and epigenetics.

When exploring the chronic stress response, I would like to talk about our vagus nerve a bit with something called the Polyvagal Theory. The Polyvagal Theory, developed by Dr. Stephen Porges, is a psychological and physiological framework that explains how the nervous system responds to stress and regulates emotional and physiological states. It emphasizes the role of the vagus nerve in controlling these responses. Some key concepts of the theory state that the vagus nerve is a major component of the parasympathetic nervous system which controls the "rest and digest" functions of the body. It then goes on to explain that there are three states of the autonomic nervous system. The first is the ventral vagal state: where we feel safe, calm, and have positive emotions. Next is the sympathetic nervous system (fight or flight): this state is activated in response to a threat and prepares you to confront danger or flee it. This state increases heart rate, blood pressure, and adrenaline. Finally, the dorsal vagal state (shutdown/freeze) when fighting or fleeing is not an option. When you have experienced childhood trauma, you can get stuck in the fight-or-flight state. This state can lead to prolonged exposure to stress hormones, which can impair immune function, increase inflammation, and raise insulin. A dysregulated immune response can then increase the risk of autoimmune conditions as well. Childhood trauma is strongly associated with mental health disorders like depression, anxiety, and PTSD, which can further influence physical health by affecting sleep, diet, and exercise patterns.

Trauma and chronic stress can cause epigenetic changes, which are modifications in gene expression without altering the DNA sequence. These changes can affect how genes related to stress response, inflammation, and immune function are expressed, potentially increasing the risk of chronic diseases.

The vagus nerve also plays an integral role in what we refer to as the gut-brain axis. In the last couple of decades, science has discovered an important link between your gut and your nervous system, earning your gut microbiome its nickname as the second brain. Many significant correlations have been drawn between stress, mood disorders, and gastrointestinal-related disorders. The gut-brain axis refers to a two-way communication pathway between the central nervous system, our brain, and the gastrointestinal tract. Our gut microbiome plays an integral role in the gut-brain axis. For example, the microorganisms in our gut directly impact the production of neurotransmitters, which are chemicals that are released from nerve cells to other target cells to communicate information. So, as you can see, our vagus nerve plays a huge role in regulating our immune system, inflammation, and gastrointestinal system.

Now, I would like to come full circle on my health story. You see, the doctors were partially right when they blamed my physical problems on being related to trauma. However, I was also correct when I kept saying I knew there was more wrong with me. However, the two were still interconnected because we are one body, and our mind, body, and soul are all connected. You can't have a sick mind and a healthy body and vice versa. The more studying I have done, the more I have concluded that my trauma put my body in constant fight-or-flight mode, and I am kind of naturally a high-strung type A personality as well, which doesn't help. Being in constant fight or flight triggered inflammation and my immune system to become dysfunctional. So, when I got bit by a tick, its bacteria threw my body into a whirlwind and triggered my immune system to get even more dysfunctional. Now, this is where epigenetics comes into play. We all have a set of genes we inherit, but that doesn't mean we are doomed by the genes we inherit. Some of the genes we would consider "bad genes" never fully express themselves. However, trauma, stress, and inflammation can change DNA and cause those bad genes to express themselves. These factors are why I started suffering more from my genetic disease called Ehlers-Danlos syndrome.

Now, I wish I could tell you I feel 100%, but I can't. What I can tell you is once I learned these things and started to feed my soul with a relationship with God, meditate, practice gratitude, and nourish my body with proper nutrients, I went from being bed-ridden, hopeless, and suicidal, to now being present in my family's life and feeling thankful and blessed. This didn't happen overnight. I started out by seeing a therapist who taught me the importance of being present in the moment. I would practice mindfulness with deep breathing exercises, gratitude journaling, and visualizations. Next, I would listen to meditation audios first thing when I would wake up, and right before bed. I also took a course in holistic nutrition. I learned that your body can't heal or function properly without the right nutrients. I also found getting out in nature helped regulate me. These tips made all the difference for me, and they can help you too! Never give up.

Melissa Cade Garcia

Founder of Transformative Connections

https://www.linkedin.com/in/melissa-cade-garcia-452a171b/
https://www.facebook.com/SHINESWF
https://www.instagram.com/transformative.connections
https://transformativeconnections.net/
http://www.amazon.com/author/melissacadegarcia

Melissa Cade Garcia is a respected expert in coaching, consulting, and education, with decades of experience empowering individuals, teams, and organizations to achieve their highest potential. She excels in leadership development and behavioral awareness, offering proven strategies to overcome challenges, build resilience, and foster authentic connections. As a Certified Coach with the John Maxwell Team and a respected DISC Consultant, Melissa provides tailored strategies to empower clients to achieve personal and professional success. Her credentials as a Behavior Analyst and Brain Health Coach, paired with a master's degree in Pastoral Counseling, allow her to approach well-being from a holistic perspective, integrating mind, body, and spirit. Melissa's dedication extends beyond her clients, as she regularly conducts training sessions and workshops through Transformative Connections, the organization she founded. With passion and insight, she inspires leaders to create transformative relationships that spark growth, connection, and long-term success in their sphere of influence.

Broken in Silence:
Healing from the Inside Out

By Melissa Cade Garcia

Have you ever felt like something inside of you was broken or missing, but you couldn't pinpoint what it was? Trauma has a way of marking every part of your life. While it is not always something you can see, its effects often linger long after the moment has passed. It shows up in small ways: subtle shifts in how we interact with others, how we view ourselves, and how we respond to the world around us. Much of the depression we see today can be traced back to the unseen wounds left behind by trauma.

Trauma is a silent force that reshapes every part of our lives, relationships, health, emotions, and spirit. It may come from a single life-altering event, like a sudden loss or accident, or from ongoing experiences such as neglect, criticism, and emotional instability. But sometimes, the hardest trauma to heal is the one you don't even recognize. When left unaddressed, these invisible burdens will fuel mental, emotional, and physical struggles, trapping us in cycles of insecurity, fear, and pain.

What many may not realize is that depression often follows unresolved trauma. In psychotherapy, depression is often described as anger turned inward. For a child, it begins to develop a quiet storm brewing beneath the surface, fueled by frustration and helplessness. It starts when the connection we were created for is disrupted or ignored, leaving the child confused and unsure. Unable to fully understand or process what is happening, they simply sense that something is wrong. Over time, that unexpressed anger and pain are buried deep inside until, one day, without warning, it erupts.

The Hidden Cost of Perfection

In my early thirties, I had worn myself ragged, trying to impress the world and prove to myself that I was someone who mattered. The turmoil and trauma of my childhood, the mental and emotional suffering of failed relationships, and the disconnect with my husband were all numbed by the massive schedule I was keeping. I threw myself into my work and responsibilities like a soldier going into battle, determined to keep going no matter the cost.

I was driven but lacked any sense of peace. A relentless voice in my head kept pushing me, whispering that I wasn't enough unless I could prove myself in every possible way. From the outside, though, my life seemed picture-perfect. A beautiful suburban home with a manicured lawn, a loving husband, and two smiling kids painted an illusion that hid the truth of the chaos within.

Balancing a forty-plus-hour workweek, full-time school, two children, a husband, a home, and an endless stream of assignments felt like stacking brick after brick on my shoulders. In rare and brief moments of pause, the weight of it all was suffocating. It left me left me questioning everything...even the existence of God. Amid the chaos, the long car rides to class became my refuge. Two or three times a week, those drives offered me the only moments of peace and solitude I could find, a brief escape from the overwhelming reality I was struggling to survive. During those trips, I clung to NPR segments, political talk shows, and Christian teaching programs. Each broadcast felt like a lifeline, offering me a short release from the burdens I willingly carried.

At the time, I wore my exhaustion like a badge of honor. In my mind, if I could keep up with this pace, even while tired, it meant I was capable, strong, and worthy. I didn't dare slow down for fear that someone might see me as weak or, worse yet, a failure. I had built a façade of control that hid the ever-growing cracks of misery underneath.

While subtle, the signs that the weight of my self-imposed obligations was taking its toll are obvious now. The bottomless cups of coffee, the sudden emotional outbursts over little things, and the bouts of sadness that would overwhelm me without notice were a few clues that things were heading in the wrong direction. But I pressed on, determined to uphold the image I had created, terrified that if I let go of even one part of the act, it would all unravel. But in my quest to keep everything together, I was slowly dying inside.

Then, in the winter of 2003, I caught the flu right after the Christmas holiday. It seemed like a fitting symbol of the coming burnout I had been neglecting for so long. While you may not be aware, one of the consequences of constant stress is a weakened immune system, so getting sick should not have been a surprise. But the flu wasn't the worst part, nor was it the aches, pains, or fever that shook me to my core. It was the shock my whole being (body, soul, and spirit) experienced all at once when I was forced to be still. For the first time in years, I had no choice but to stop.

Lying almost paralyzed in my bed, I felt powerless. Everything I had worked so hard to control was now out of reach. My busy schedule came to an unplanned and abrupt halt. For the first time in maybe forever, I was alone with myself...alone with my thoughts. In that stillness, and over the next few days, the floodgates opened, and every issue I had been pretending didn't exist came rushing to the surface. The emotions, the pain, the memories I had worked so hard to suppress, everything I thought I could keep hidden, came pouring out. It was like a broken dam, overwhelmed by intense rainfall. It was a storm, a storm that overwhelmed me all at once.

As it turns out, I had instinctively learned to hide my pain in my childhood. I discovered that vulnerability was something to be feared, and emotions were a weakness I could not afford. Instead of feeling and acknowledging the hurt, I detached from it. It was a survival skill I had picked up to keep out the unrest of growing up in my home. My soul welled up with pride to protect me, and I was convinced I was strong and didn't need anyone. I told myself I was perfect just as I was, independent and untouched by the chaos that had shaped my earlier years. But the truth was, I wasn't perfect. I was broken.

My mind's defense mechanism had been to shut off the emotions, to build walls so high that I could go through the motions of life without anyone, including myself, noticing the cracks beneath the surface. I had mastered the art of pretending and suppressing my emotions. I was so good at it, in fact, that I had forgotten how to feel. And so, for years, I wore the mask of perfection. That is, until my body and mind refused to cooperate any longer.

Understanding the Impact of Trauma on Our Body, Soul, and Spirit

Through my studies in human behavior and pastoral counseling coursework, I gained a deeper understanding of childhood trauma and the profound effects it has physically, emotionally, and spiritually. To help you grasp why my world (and perhaps yours) suddenly unraveled, it is essential to explore the makeup of humanity. Every person consists of three parts: body, soul, and spirit.

The *body* is the most tangible aspect of our being, easily understood because we can see it in the reflection of a mirror. It is made up of our cells, nerves, bones, brain, and other organs. This part of us ages a little each day and, no matter how well we care for it, will eventually stop functioning. Our body *connects us to the world* around us through our five senses: sight, smell, hearing, taste, and touch. These "gates" allow us to experience and engage with life.

The *soul*, however, is where we *connect with ourselves*, and find the desire to belong. It encompasses our mind, will, and emotions, shaping our thoughts, beliefs, memories, values, attitudes, and feelings, which many refer to as the subconscious mind. Essentially, our soul defines our personality and is deeply influenced by our environment, life experiences (both positive and negative), upbringing, education, and culture. Often seen as the protector of the person, the soul serves as the director of both the body and spirit. With the power of will, it becomes the decision-making center, even when we are not fully aware of the choices being made.

At the core of our being lies the *spirit*. This is the part of us that seeks *connection with our Creator* and holds us accountable. The spirit governs our reasoning and conscience, guiding our sense of right and wrong. It is also linked to our intuition, allowing us to "know" something without physical evidence or external input. The spirit gives us life and is believed to represent the highest level of human functioning when we connect with God. Without that connection, we carry an emptiness often referred to as a "God-shaped hole" within us.

Together, the body, soul, and spirit form our whole being, each part playing a crucial and interwoven role in shaping who we are. However, in the broken world we live in, we inevitably encounter broken people through our relationships. Our soul deeply desires healthy connections, to be loved and accepted, and to feel that we truly matter. Unfortunately, we often experience wounds and scars inflicted by the sharp edges of those who bring the opposite into our lives. More often than not, it comes from the people we love the most. In an effort to protect ourselves from future trauma, our soul collaborates with our body to create defense mechanisms.

My parents' lives were shaped by deep trauma suffered through neglect, abandonment, and emotional, verbal, and physical abuse. Tragically, this traumatic rejection came from the very people who were supposed to love them the most. Both were the eldest in their families. Mom was the oldest of nine children, and Dad, after losing his older brother, became the eldest of thirteen. Being the firstborn naturally placed them in positions of responsibility, which, only combined with the harsh environments they grew up in, shaped their strong and dominant personalities.

It is no surprise that their unresolved pain followed them into their marriage, creating a chaotic and intense home environment. Both Mom and Dad were young, determined, and strong-willed, which often led to explosive arguments that sometimes turned physical. For a young child, this was deeply confusing. A child caught in the crossfire has no idea how to navigate the volatile shifting dynamics in the home. How do you reconcile loving your parents while feeling fear and unease because of their actions? The very people meant to provide safety were also the source of instability. Emotionally, I was caught in a whirlwind of conflicting feelings. Unsure of how to process or navigate them, I was left to struggle with a lost sense of identity and security.

Mom and Dad's unhealed wounds of rejection brought an emotional rawness to their relationship and, in some ways, limited their ability to fully express love. For me, while I did not know it at the time, growing up in this environment impacted me deeply. It shaped how I understood relationships, love, and security from a very early age. But the effects didn't stop there; they shaped me in ways that took years to understand and heal from.

Beyond the Surface

In order to break free from depression requires understanding the connection between our body, soul, and spirit and how trauma affects our central nervous system. To truly grasp how our past hurts shape who we are today, allow me to get a little geeky with you, and dive a little deeper into the science behind it. Childhood trauma has a profound impact on our bodies, causing reactions similar to those within our souls. These reactions take place within our central nervous system, which consists of two parts.

The first part is the **sympathetic system**, responsible for giving us the energy to work hard and keep going. It is activated during times of stress or danger, preparing the body for the "fight or flight" reaction known to almost every human. Think of it as the "go, go, go" engine in your body. When activated, this system increases your heart rate, slows your digestion, dilates your pupils, and releases **adrenaline** and **cortisol.** These are known as the stress hormones. *Adrenaline* provides a burst of energy, while *cortisol* helps you stay alert during prolonged periods of stress. In the soul, emotionally, the sympathetic system reflects feelings such as anxiety, fear, or determination.

Essentially, this sympathetic system protects you by helping the body react quickly under stressful conditions. Scientists say that it was particularly helpful when our ancestors lived off the land and in the wilderness. For example, if a person ran into a tiger while hunting for dinner, the sympathetic system would kick into gear, preparing them to either flee or stay and defend themselves. In a modernized world, we no longer face those types of dangers. However, to the nervous system, danger is danger, no matter how it appears.

To balance this intense system, we were blessed with the **parasympathetic system**, which helps to calm the body down after stress. Its job is to bring the body back to a relaxed state, to help it recover. This is the rest, healing, and restorative piece of our nervous system. It does this by slowing down the heart rate, promoting digestion, constricting the pupils, and assisting the body in conserving energy. Known also as the "rest and digest" system, it allows the body to heal from stressful situations. This state reflects the spirit's connection to God and can lead the soul and body into a place of rest.

The way the body functions is an absolute miracle. For a child to grow into a healthy, well-functioning adult, their nervous system must be in balance. However, if that child grows up in a chaotic environment, where the body senses danger more often than not, the child spends most of their time in a constant state of alert, dominated by the sympathetic nervous system. In healthy homes, children learn from their caregivers how to adjust their nervous system through experiences that promote safety, connection, and calmness. Over time, as the child encounters more opportunities in the home that make them feel safe, mentally, emotionally, and physically the parasympathetic system grows stronger. But what happens if that is not the case?

Consider a five-year-old child who witnesses their parents' argument escalate into a violent confrontation. What do you suppose happens inside her innocent mind and body? As part of the soul, the mind, will, and emotions come into play. The child hears the yelling and sees the violent behavior, sending signals to the brain that danger is present. She feels an overwhelming sense of fear because the two people who usually keep her safe are acting erratically. The sympathetic nervous system kicks in and prepares for "fight or flight." Her heart rate rises in an effort to supply her muscles with oxygen in case she needs to run or defend herself. Then, the body floods with the stress hormones. The rush of adrenaline causes the young child to feel restless, hyper-alert, and shaky, while the cortisol heightens her awareness, all in an attempt to survive the situation. Sadly, many children will tend to internalize the conflict. It will leave them wondering what they did wrong or if they could have prevented what happened by behaving better, shaping their thinking for life.

The Cost of Constant Chaos

Surprisingly, witnessing violent altercations in childhood is not the only experience that produces these results. When a parent is absent, perpetually busy, or consumed by their own chaos, it can lead to similar effects on the child's mind and body. We were created for connection, and when that is lacking in the life of the child, though not violent in nature, it can cause uncertainty in the soul, and create the feeling of not belonging. A young child is not yet equipped to process these confusing events and emotions on their own. Their yearning for care, connection, and comfort is intrinsic. If these things are lacking and there is no intervention, it will shape their understanding of love, conflict, and security, often scarring them for life.

In such situations, children may feel they must constantly prove their worth, so they are always on guard, striving harder, seeking validation, or earning approval. Their sympathetic nervous system remains in overdrive, continuously releasing stress hormones like adrenaline and cortisol to cope with the perceived threats of life. While young bodies are initially equipped to handle this, prolonged exposure to stress without recovery drains these resources, preventing the body and mind from ever reaching a state of true rest.

This persistent state of stress not only affects the body but also reshapes who the child was meant to be. Their body and mind become programmed to always be on alert, scanning for danger, even when it does not exist. This means they are unknowingly in a constant state of stress. In effect, their sympathetic system regularly releases adrenaline and cortisol in order to handle life. When we are younger, we have plenty of resources stored in our body. However, too much exposure, with a lack of recovery time, never allows one's mind to truly rest because the body is not given time to rest and relax.

Emotionally, it shapes the child's belief system. The child will likely develop emotional regulation issues making it harder for them to process their feelings or calm down after an upsetting situation. As adults, they may default to "fight, flight, or freeze" responses: lashing out aggressively, avoiding situations or people that remind them of past trauma, or withdrawing entirely in fear.

At age five, witnessing violence can alter the brain's development. The prefrontal cortex, the area responsible for decision-making and self-control, may weaken, making the child more prone to anxious thoughts and impulsive behavior. If such experiences are severe or ongoing, unresolved patterns can cause the child to perceive the world as inherently unsafe, resulting in emotional and physical challenges that extend into adulthood.

The consequences are far-reaching. The chronic stress can lead to anxiety, irritability, sleep disturbances, weight gain, a weakened immune system, and many other ailments. Like a new car that runs great in the beginning, but never gets serviced or has its oil changed, the body that unknowingly never rests will eventually burn out.

Depression can stem from various causes, but in this case, it emerges as the body's way of slowing down after years of overexertion, almost as if it is forcing it to rest. Of course, the fact that we have depleted our body of energy and denied it the rest it needs to function properly only adds to this depressive state. When this happens, the parasympathetic system attempts to restore balance, forcing the body to pause and recover.

What I have come to understand is that pretending not to care, while seemingly protective, only serves to mask our true selves. Over time, this pretense not only disconnects us from our authentic identity but also prevents us from healing and growing into the person we were always meant to be. Confronting and processing these emotions is an important step toward moving forward, healing, and reclaiming who we were always meant to be.

Depression is far more than just feeling sad; it is an all-consuming weight, one that is almost impossible to put into words unless you've lived through it yourself. I vividly remember one morning when the depth of it hit me hardest. I woke up, only to be met with a devastating sense of dread and disappointment, knowing I had to face yet another day. While I did not have thoughts of harming myself, in my soul, I knew that death was the only way to escape the suffocating hopelessness that had consumed me over the last few weeks. As I tried to muster the strength to get out of bed, I instead collapsed onto the floor, curling into the fetal position, overcome by despair.

For those who have not experienced it, depression is a relentless force that touches every part of your being – body, soul, and spirit. Your body is fatigued, your appetite fades, your sleep patterns are interrupted, and your judgment is clouded with confusion and self-doubt. Feelings of worthlessness and despair are magnified beyond comprehension, accompanied by the most harsh and self-defeating dialogue you have ever heard, exacerbating the hopelessness and disconnect you are already experiencing. It feels inescapable, creating a vicious cycle that deepens the darkness you are in.

In what became the most desperate moment of my life, I found myself lying on the floor, tears streaming down my face as uncontrollable sobs shook my whole body. In that very vulnerable state, I cried out, begging the same Creator I had questioned even existed just a few months earlier. "God help me!" What happened next is something I can only describe as divine intervention, a moment that still feels almost unbelievable even twenty-one years later.

First, I heard a voice, not audibly, but clearly and deep within my spirit. It was unmistakably different from my own thoughts. The words came clearly: "If you want to continue to live your life without Me, this is what it feels like." Strangely, those words did not bring me fear or confusion. Instead, they overwhelmed me with a sense of peace and clarity, only intensifying my emotions. It was true I had been running my life entirely on my own terms, striving to make myself look good. I had placed myself at the center, living as though I were the god of my own life. And yet, what an empty and unfulfilling life it was. I could not stand to be alone with my own thoughts because I could not face the reality of what was.

Immediately following that, I saw a vivid image flash through my mind: the faces of my children, just six and ten years old at the time. In that instant, everything shifted. It was a turning point that marked the beginning of a profound change in my life's perspective. It was as if I was pulled far back, far enough to see the true blessings I had been missing. My eyes were instantly off of me, and I pondered the question, "What would happen to my children if they lost their mother?"

There was no miraculous healing from my depression in that instant, but I got up off the floor differently than when I went down. In that moment, I laid down the arrogant pride that had falsely shielded me and fully surrendered to God—soul, body, and spirit. Let me be clear: Healing was a process. I began to realize that every part of me needed restoration, from the deep wounds of childhood trauma to the self-inflicted damage of my choices. All of it had contributed to the disconnection within me that led to the overwhelming depression I faced on that cold December morning in Florida.

Yet, here is the beautiful truth: the same connection with God that I had been avoiding held the power to heal. It was the key to leading me back to the person I was always meant to be—whole, free, and full of purpose.

Holistic Healing: Body, Soul, and Spirit

Where I am today is far from where I found myself over two decades ago. While my life is not perfect, I am deeply grateful for how far I have come. Breaking the cycle of pain and disconnection began with acknowledging the storm I had spent years trying to suppress, along with the physical damage and chemical imbalance I had created in an attempt to outrun it all. It took hitting rock bottom for me to realize that I was not just a body going through the motions or a soul longing for belonging, I was a spirit in desperate need of healing.

Being a reader and researcher at heart, I leaned into what I did best and began to learn about the causes of depression. Perhaps the greatest revelation was that my depression was multi-faceted. Healing did not come overnight, nor was it a single event. It was a medley of therapies that required intention, patience, and grace. I had to address all parts of my being – spirit, soul, and body – each one intricately connected to the others. Rebuilding required learning how to care for my body, confront and reframe my inner thoughts, and nurture my spirit.

Over time, I discovered the transformative power of self-compassion and self-connection. These practices and principles helped me reconnect with myself, with God, and with the purpose I was created for. Let me share what I learned, in the hope that it might guide you toward your own healing and wholeness.

The Spirit

Taking care of your spirit looks different for everyone. While all three parts work together to create a whole and healed human, the spirit gives life and holds our true identity. As a person of faith, I came to understand that God created me to be me. Through complete surrender to His will, I discovered a genuine confidence, one that came from trusting Him with every aspect of my life and being. This is the kind of confidence that is rooted in acceptance and the understanding that I am not defined by my past, but by the Creator who designed me with a plan and a purpose.

I embraced the truth that the experiences of my past, especially those that deprived me of the love and connection I was meant to receive, shaped false beliefs about who I truly was. The early wounds led me to adopt an identity that was not in line with my true self. I needed restoration, the kind that freed me from the lies I had believed for so long. God created me to be me, not someone else. Not someone who shrinks back from the world to avoid being hurt again, and not someone who becomes callous and suspicious of others. Both of these were ways of rejecting the real me, the person God designed.

God has an abundant plan for your life, but in order to embrace it, you must first uncover what lies hidden beneath the mask you've worn for protection. In my case, growth and restoration began through prayer, reading the Scriptures, and finding a supportive community that supported me and my growth.

Prayer strengthens your connection with God, allowing you to hear His voice more clearly and seek His guidance. The Word of God is a powerful tool that shapes your mind, brings truth to your soul, and helps you break free from the lies you have believed. And a community that shares your values can provide encouragement, accountability, and a safe place to grow. Only then can you begin to step into the fullness of who you were always meant to be.

The Body

During the period when I was struggling with depression, it just so happened that school was on recess. With my class load reduced and my full-time internship about to begin, my schedule became more flexible. I knew that both my mental and physical state needed attention, and I was determined to make a change. Without the car rides to class that had once provided me with moments of solitude, I had to create those moments for myself.

Despite my dislike for both exercise and being alone with my thoughts, I committed to walking in my neighborhood for at least twenty minutes a day, four or five times a week. I had learned that it would help to reduce my stress levels and improve my mood. Apparently, my chronic stress levels, combined with my lack of exercise, caused an interruption or a lack of the production of good hormones, such as serotonin, dopamine, and endorphins. During these walks, I took the time to converse with God, allowing Him to speak to my heart. Slowly, those quiet moments began to strengthen my spirit and bring clarity to my mind.

My diet also needed to change. For too long, I had been relying on fast food and coffee to fuel my body. Another lesson I learned is that poor nutrition can affect your mood and brain health. I became more intentional about what I was eating, understanding that proper nutrition could support the clarity and resilience I needed in my mind. Today, I still drink coffee, but in moderation, fast food is rare, if ever something that I have for a meal.

As for my sleep, it was a mess. I made a conscious effort to try and get proper rest each night. But if you have ever battled depression, you know that healthy sleep doesn't always come easily. Sometimes, it's all you want to do, and other times, it just doesn't cooperate. Maneuvering a full schedule, with assignments always due, I had pulled a lot of all-nighters, often only getting three to four hours of sleep. While my high levels of cortisol created by my stress made this possible, the constant release also disrupted the important "feel-good" chemicals produced in my brain.

I decided to see a doctor, and to this day, I believe it was a divine appointment. This doctor and his wife were temporarily in my area, as their hearts were devoted to missionary work. They both prayed for me, and he prescribed a small dose of an antidepressant as he had diagnosed me as clinically depressed. He assured me it would be a temporary solution, just enough time to help stabilize my mood and sleep patterns. After about a year, he was able to gradually wean me off the medication. Not long after, he and his wife moved to South America to continue their missionary work.

The Soul

The soul is the part of you that holds your mind, will, and emotions. Think of it as the driver's seat for your decisions and the place where your thoughts and feelings live. Healing starts here. Often, it begins with a gentle nudge from your spirit, urging you to make the decision to heal. But here's the thing: It takes commitment, real, honest commitment, as well as a willingness to face the parts of yourself you have been avoiding and ignoring for years. It is in your soul, aligned with your spirit, that you will find the courage to take off the mask you have been wearing for so long and finally deal with the wounds and disconnection that have kept you from experiencing peace and wholeness.

Now, this healing path looks different for everyone, but it will always start in the same place, identifying the cause of your pain and unrest. Once you believe you are ready, this means carving out time to sit and quietly reflect. I know it sounds intimidating, but it is necessary. Think back to what you have been through, what you remember, and what you feel. Be honest with yourself. It is not easy, but it is important.

Here is where it gets harder: You have to let it go. Letting go involves forgiveness – forgiveness of yourself and others. By no means does this excuse the harm that was done to you, but it does have the capacity to free you from the hold it has had on your peace of mind.

Now, let me make an important point on forgiveness: It often does not stick the first time. In fact, it is more of a practice because of the humanity in our souls. It wants to continue to protect you. This is because the anger behind unforgiveness gives you a false sense of power, and is often considered a weakness by society. The truth is that forgiveness is one of the most valuable and strong actions a former victim can take.

That is where your spirit comes in. For me, turning to God made the impossible feel possible. I started to see that people who hurt others are often carrying their own unhealed wounds. Whether it was through words, actions, or neglect, their brokenness impacted their ability to love and connect. Understanding this doesn't excuse their behavior, but it can help you start the process of forgiveness, and break the cycle that has been holding you back.

In some cases, especially when the pain feels too deep to face alone, seeking professional counseling can be a helpful step. Counseling can guide you through the healing process in a safe and supportive way. Alongside this, practicing gratitude and self-compassion can lay a stronger foundation for your journey. Being kind to yourself and intentionally focusing on the beauty and abundance around you can transform a negative perspective into one that sees blessings and hope. Gratitude has a way of opening your eyes to the goodness already present in your life, even during hard times. Keeping a gratitude journal is a great tool for this.

As I began my faith journey, this shift in perspective made the painful process of healing a little easier. It built a deep trust in God's plan for my life, which gave me the courage to keep moving forward. That trust opened my eyes to the people in my life who were sent as blessings, and it allowed me to cherish them more deeply. It also opened the door to discovering who I was truly meant to be.

It is not about erasing the past; it's about reclaiming your power over it. Remember this: You may be broken, but not beyond repair. Even in your darkest moments, you are still worthy of peace, love, and purpose. Trauma may have left its marks on your life, but those marks do not define you. As a part of your story, you have everything you need inside of you to choose how that story will end. Choose healing and growth...discover who you were always meant to be.

Bibliography

Cade Garcia, Melissa. *The Power of Self-Connection: A Transformative Self-Help Guide, Workbook, Journal, & Dedicated Gratitude Log.* Transformative Connections, 2024.

Cade Garcia, Melissa. *The Reality of Rejection: It Is Real. It Is Painful. It Is Ugly...But It Never Has to Define Your Life Again!* Transformative Connections, 2023.

Marieb, Elaine N., and Katja Hoehn. *Human Anatomy & Physiology.* 11th ed., Pearson Education, 2018.

McEwen, Bruce S., and John C. Wingfield. "The Concept of Allostasis in Biology and Biomedicine." *Hormones and Behavior*, vol. 43, no. 1, 2003, pp. 2–15.

Osofsky, Joy D. "The Effects of Exposure to Violence on Young Children." *Children in a Violent Society*, edited by Joy D. Osofsky, Guilford Press, 1997, pp. 9–25.

Scazzero, Peter. *Emotionally Healthy Spirituality: It's Impossible to Be Spiritually Mature, While Remaining Emotionally Immature.* Zondervan, 2014.

Stahl, Stephen M. *Stahl's Essential Psychopharmacology: Neuroscientific Basis and Practical Applications.* Cambridge University Press, 2021.

Aliesha Pollino

CEO of Pollino Health & Wellness

https://www.facebook.com/profile.php?id=9340891
https://linktr.ee/aliesha.pollino

Aliesha Pollino, CEO of Pollino Health & Wellness, is a #1 international bestselling author, intuitive transformation coach, and public speaker passionate about empowering women to heal, rediscover their dreams, and step into their most authentic selves. With a multifaceted approach to wellness, she guides clients through mental, physical, emotional, and financial healing, helping them cultivate self-love and purpose.

Beyond her work, Aliesha finds joy as a devoted dog mom to her spirited Australian Shepherd, Lexie, and takes pride in being an aunt and godmother to seven incredible children. Her adventurous spirit fuels a love for the outdoors, including hunting, fishing, and exploring nature, while her passion for travel inspires new perspectives and personal growth.

Driven by resilience and self-empowerment, Aliesha serves as a guiding light for those ready to transform their lives, helping them break free from limitations and create a life they're excited to wake up to every day.

From Doing to Being: Embracing the Journey to My True Purpose

By Aliesha Pollino

The Mind Can Be a Dark Place

Lost in a dense forest, I spun in circles, searching for footprints to retrace. Snow fell in thick, heavy flakes, quickly turning into a whiteout. I wasn't dressed for this. Panic set in—no shelter, no sense of direction. My breath caught, my chest tightened—then suddenly, I jolted awake.

Heart pounding, I stared at my phone. 3:30 a.m. The dream lingered, unsettling. Instead of relief, my thoughts spiraled.

How are you almost 40 and still don't have it together?

Remember when you thought you'd have life figured out by 30? Another decade is slipping away—what happened to the dream job, the house, the perfect family?

By 5:30 a.m., I felt like I was being tortured. I couldn't lie there stuck in my thoughts anymore. My mind was dragging me down a rabbit hole of unmet expectations. So, I got up, grabbed my never-ending to-do list, and distracted myself with busy work.

Later, I had a Zoom call with a group of faith-driven women entrepreneurs. I didn't want to show up. I felt like I didn't belong—not accomplished, strong, or faithful enough. But I had committed, so I logged on.

When it was my turn to speak, I prayed for time to run out. Instead, the host asked about my life, something about God—and suddenly, tears streamed down my face. I confessed to a group of strangers how lost I felt, like I was trapped in a shaken snow globe, unable to see my next step.

After the call, I couldn't shake how similar the snow globe analogy was to that dream. It hit me like a ton of bricks: my subconscious was screaming for attention. *Have you ever felt like you were standing in a snow globe, unsure which way to go?*

That moment of vulnerability marked the beginning of an inward journey—to finally confront what had kept me stuck and step into the life I truly desired.

The Darkness Beneath the Surface

From the outside, I looked successful—checking off milestones: school, career, marriage (then divorce), business ownership. People assumed I had it all together, but inside, I never felt enough, always chasing an unattainable version of myself.

By 2020, I hit rock bottom again. Despite two back surgeries, chronic pain persisted, and my doctor warned a third might be inevitable. The thought was soul-crushing. One night, overwhelmed, I opened my phone's notes app and wrote my end-of-life requests. *God, if I have to go under the knife again, take me on the table. End the pain. End the burden I've become.*

Desperate, I threw myself into another diet, hoping weight loss would ease the pain. I forced daily walks, whispering to my dog through tears: I can do it. You can do it. We can do it. After two months and just five pounds lost, nothing changed. It felt like a never-ending nightmare.

Then, one sleepless night, I saw a Facebook reel of people holding signs with their weight loss numbers. It wasn't the numbers that struck me—it was the light in their eyes. They looked alive. Clinging to a drop of hope, I reached out to a coach.

That decision changed everything. Yes, I lost 103 pounds and 96.5 inches. But more importantly, I gained my life back. I went from surviving to thriving—something I never thought possible. Strength training became essential, not just for fitness but to stay functional despite nerve damage in my leg and foot. One month into my journey, I knew I had to help others, and Pollino Health & Wellness was born.

But transformation isn't a one-time event—it's a lifelong journey. Just when I thought I had overcome my biggest hurdles, life threw new challenges my way.

The Whisper of Change

For the first time, I wasn't just maintaining weight loss—I had truly broken the cycle. I finally understood not just how to lose weight but how to keep it off. Yet, by fall 2022, new health challenges left me drained, struggling to keep up with my busy life.

At the same time, I was expanding my business into a holistic model rooted in mind, body, and spirit. I had learned that true transformation isn't just about nutrition or exercise—it requires mental and spiritual alignment. For years, I yo-yo dieted and overexerted myself, ignoring deeper struggles. I'd tell myself, I'm fine! while sweeping issues under the rug. Breaking that cycle showed me I could help others do the same.

As 2024 began—the year I'd turn 40—I reflected on these shifts. I had always dreamed of writing a book, but I kept attaching 'someday' to it. That changed after that emotional Zoom call with my women's group. One woman later invited me to contribute a chapter to an anthology. My first thought? Didn't you hear the 'someday' I tacked onto that dream? She dismissed it: There's no better way to start than dipping your toe in the pond. Writing just one chapter felt manageable, so I agreed.

As I wrote about my aunt's murder, something unexpected happened—my long-dormant spiritual gifts reawakened. I had always been sensitive to energy, easily overwhelmed in crowds as a child. I had shut that part of myself down for years, but now, amid healing, it felt like the floodgates had opened. It was overwhelming, even suffocating, and I wondered: Could these gifts be strengths?

People often told me to slow down, fearing burnout. I wanted to scream, *If I don't do it, who will?* My days blurred into meetings, deadlines, and solving everyone else's problems—all while chasing a multi-million-dollar empire and a balanced life. I wore my busyness as a badge of honor, but a growing whisper urged me to pause, breathe, and listen.

Then one day, I realized I couldn't recall a single thing I had done all day. It freaked me out. My body was screaming for rest, but slowing down terrified me. Days later, I found myself sobbing in my doctor's office, fearing my health issues would destroy everything—my business, relationships, life. I agreed to a temporary medication for focus and energy, but I knew it wasn't a long-term fix.

I had to face the truth: in chasing goals and taking care of everyone else, I had forgotten how to simply exist. I began asking myself two life-changing questions:

Who are you?

Are you truly walking in your purpose?

I had two choices: stay stuck in the storm or step into the unknown. Staying stuck felt like being lost in a whiteout—exposed, at risk of losing everything. But moving forward was the only way to finally break through.

Stepping Into the Unknown

The unknown is terrifying. It demanded me to step out of the comfort zones that kept me tethered to survival but starved of growth. For years, I survived by people-pleasing and clinging to the belief that I wasn't enough—that love was something to earn, and happiness was beyond my reach or something I didn't truly deserve.

I grew tired of waking up disconnected from the woman I knew I could be and tired of replaying the same patterns that left me feeling unfulfilled and unseen. It was time for change, even if it meant stepping into uncharted territory.

Small Steps, Big Shifts

Change didn't happen overnight. I started with small, intentional steps that wouldn't overwhelm my already overflowing to-do list. I leaned into faith, rediscovering my connection with God and learning more about Jesus' life and service by reading a few pages of the Bible at least three times a week. Gratitude became my anchor. Each morning, before my feet touched the floor, I listed three things I was thankful for—sometimes simple, like brushing my teeth or having air in my lungs, and other times profound, like the ability to love and serve others. Whether it was simple or profound, each day, I found new things to be grateful for.

I also began taking inventory of my life: what filled my cup and what drained it. What made me feel good and what made me feel bad. I made a running list of people, places, and habits and added them to the appropriate columns on my sheet. This awareness shaped how I spent my time and energy.

By May, I thought I was making progress. I felt strong enough to ask my doctor about tapering off my medication, which I hated relying on. He agreed, and we created a plan to reduce my dose. But I wasn't prepared for what followed.

The Meltdown

Mid-May felt like a dumpster fire. My energy tanked, and despite endless cups of coffee and energy drinks, I couldn't keep myself awake. My emotions spiraled; my mind went back to not being able to hold a thought. It wasn't until a friend connected the dots between my symptoms and the medication reduction that I realized what was happening. After reinstating my original dose, my body slowly stabilized, but not before I hit yet another rock bottom.

One night, I was desperate for a hug, not just any hug or one that just anyone can give you. *A hug so strong, so tight, that you feel safe enough to take off the armor you had been wearing to be strong and just be able to rest.*

No one was there. I sobbed, asking, *God, why I didn't have that kind of person in my life to give me that kind of hug*? I spent that night cuddling my dog and ultimately holding myself—literally wrapping my arms around my own body in a desperate attempt to feel some resemblance of comfort and safety. My body felt like it was betraying me, barely functioning like it was on the edge of giving up on me. I questioned whether I would wake up the next morning, whether my lungs would still carry breath, or if my body would simply stop.

The next morning, when I opened my eyes, I realized that I had pulled myself out of one of the darkest mental moments of my life yet again. It wasn't anyone else who saved me; it was me. That realization planted a seed deep within me.

I spent the rest of that month peeling back layers of my fears, doubts, and insecurities. With each layer I uncovered, I found a profound truth: I was enough. I didn't need someone else to save me, and I didn't need anyone else to create a sense of safety for me. That power, that security, could only come from within me.

This shift in perspective was subtle at first, but it became the foundation for what came next: the steppingstones to rebuild my life with a renewed sense of purpose, self-worth, and alignment.

A Shift in Perspective

The following months were pivotal in my journey. Instead of fearing the unknown, I embraced it. I reframed questions like "Who are you?" and "Are you living your purpose?" as opportunities to explore my soul's calling.

I knew the journey required:

- Openness to change
- Dedication to balance work and rest
- A support system—I couldn't do it alone and needed guidance
- Courage to face hard truths, knowing some days would make me want to quit
- Continued advocacy for my health

Around this time, I found a holistic doctor in Texas, recommended by a friend. After submitting my tests, I anxiously awaited our Zoom call. She started with: "I don't know how you're not in a coma yet." Wait—coma? My thyroid had essentially stopped working, and my T4 wasn't converting to T3. My T3 levels were critically low. The doctor explained that brain function and memory would be one of the last things to fail before a coma. I was overwhelmed—angry, scared, but also relieved. Finally, someone validated my struggles. It wasn't ideal, but I knew it would be okay once I found the right combination of medication.

With renewed hope, I set a clear intention. I wrote in my journal: 'I am calling in the mentors, guides, and opportunities that will help me step fully into my purpose.' And then, I let go. I trusted. Within days, the right people started showing up—conversations, connections, invitations. It was as if the universe had been waiting for me to surrender. Manifestation isn't about control; it's about alignment. The more I let go, the faster the right doors opened. While the path was unclear in the beginning, with every step, a light appeared to show the way to the next step.

Facing Myself

Unraveling the layers of who I was—and who I wasn't—was the hardest part. I had to let go of roles and expectations that no longer served me. Surrender was a word that quickly became a theme of the summer if I was going to see true change in my life.

Prior to this year, most people would probably classify me as a super type A person. What I realized was that the super type A personality I created was because of all of the pain and hurt I had experienced in my life from people and external environments. Needing to have all the information and all the details about everything allowed me to have a feeling of control or, in a sense, to feel safe.

Through surrender I realized I was actually more of *gypsy soul*—free-spirited, adventurous, and go-with-the-flow mentality. I have a love for travel and exploration, and a deep appreciation for the beauty of life and nature.

For as long as I could remember, my worth had been tied to productivity. If I wasn't constantly doing, I felt like I was failing. Slowing down felt like weakness, like I was falling behind. But as I dove deeper into my healing, I realized something profound—so many of the limiting beliefs I carried weren't even mine to begin with. They had been passed down, absorbed from the world around me, ingrained in my identity without me ever questioning them.

At first, the idea of simply being—of allowing myself to exist without proving, fixing, or striving—felt unbearable. Who was I if I wasn't accomplishing something? The silence, the stillness, felt like a void I wasn't ready to face. Thankfully, my incredible team of mentors and guides reminded me that the kind of inner work I was doing wasn't for the faint of heart. Releasing old patterns, rewiring my mind, and embracing a new way of living required energy—energy I barely had to spare, given my ongoing health challenges.

But in surrendering control, something unexpected happened. Letting go of fear, scarcity, and the belief that I had to earn my place in the world freed me to take bolder, more aligned steps in my life. Instead of chasing after an external sense of worth, I began creating a life I truly loved waking up to.

Now, my mornings look different. Instead of waking up and diving into my to-do list, I start my day with intention. Before my feet even touch the floor, I place my hand over my heart, take a deep breath, and say, 'Today, I allow myself to just be.' I no longer measure success by productivity. Some days, being fully present with my dog, feeling the warmth of the sun on my face, or simply listening to my intuition is enough. The need to prove, hustle, and overachieve? It no longer controls me.

My Business

When I started my business in 2020, I approached it with the mindset that I wanted to help anyone and everyone. However, as I connected with potential clients, I realized that not everyone was truly ready for the life-changing journey I was offering. Some were seeking quick fixes—a band-aid for deeper issues they weren't ready to address. Out of fear and a scarcity mindset, I said "yes" to anyone, even when it didn't feel aligned.

Because I pour my heart into every client's journey, I found myself emotionally drained when they gave up on themselves. I wanted them to see the potential I saw in them, but their lack of trust in themselves made me feel like I was failing. The same was true for the individuals I partnered with to teach others; while their successes were their own, I took their failures personally.

Then came a turning point that might sound crazy to other business owners: I started firing clients. I began interviewing potential clients as much as they were interviewing me. If it didn't feel like the right fit, I wouldn't take them on. I'll never forget the first time I turned someone down—I thought, *Did I just say no to helping someone and no to making money?* But the feeling was liberating.

Letting go of clients who weren't ready created space for those who truly wanted change. It was scary at first, but surrendering to this process transformed my business. Now, I'm attracting clients who are committed to doing the work, and the depth of our conversations and their breakthroughs have been incredible. Watching them awaken and rediscover themselves fills my heart and aligns me with my purpose.

I've also embraced a new mindset about success: I can create a thriving business, earn money, and make a meaningful impact. My work is important, and I'm proud to stand confidently in my power as both a coach and a business owner.

My Relationships: Personal & Professional

For most of my life, I was a people-pleaser, clinging to the belief that I wasn't enough—that love had to be earned, and happiness was out of reach. I thought boundaries meant telling someone, *you can't treat me this way anymore.* Now, I understand that boundaries aren't about controlling others; they're about my response.

I've learned to say "no" without guilt, take time for self-care without feeling selfish, and I'm allowed to change my mind without offering a lengthy explanation. I honor my peace by removing myself from situations, people, or places that don't feel right, and I no longer feel the need to justify my choices. This newfound clarity has transformed both my personal and professional relationships.

Awakening My Gifts

At the start of summer, I believed spiritual gifts were an either-or situation—you either connected with those who had passed or worked with energy, but not both. I assumed gifts fit into neat categories; each person assigned just one.

For as long as I can remember, my gift has been feeling energy—from people, the departed, nature, animals, and everything in between. I don't often see spirits in physical form, but I sense their presence in a way that is just as real. With guidance from a mentor, I learned that my gifts require me to slow down, be present, and simply be—a lesson that felt both foreign and necessary. Like any form of growth, this process is about progress, not perfection—it unfolds in its own time.

Through months of deep inner work, I came to understand that gifts aren't either-or—they can be both-and. My connection has expanded in ways I never imagined. Now, spirits communicate with me in different forms—some appear visually, while others come as colors, sensations, or pure energy. I've also developed a deeper, more intuitive ability to shift and move energy, both within myself and for others.

As I began working with energy, everything changed. Clearing emotional and energetic blocks helped me break cycles I had been stuck in for years. My intuition sharpened, guiding me in ways logic never could. Clients started coming to me, not just for health coaching, but because they could feel something different—a deeper transformation happening beneath the surface. Energy work wasn't just something I did; it became a key part of how I help others step into their power.

Navigating Setbacks

By September, I felt like my world was crashing down again. Blood work revealed my T3 levels had dropped significantly lower than they were in June, and the generic medication wasn't effective. Transitioning to a brand-name prescription in October helped, but the delay took a toll.

October was also challenging because I was diving deeper into my spiritual growth, experiencing the so-called "ascension flu." This journey has been far from linear. Setbacks happen, but each time I return to myself, I gain more clarity, peace, and freedom.

I've realized that awakening isn't a destination—it's a daily practice. It's about aligning with my truth, choosing myself, and embracing the power of simply *being*.

Healing Powers of Nature

October was also a month of profound breakthroughs. I began uncovering the core of who I am, and nature became my anchor. It's in nature that I feel most grounded and whole. For me, hunting and fishing aren't just hobbies—they're essential practices that recharge my spirit and help me reconnect with myself.

As my new medications started to take effect and archery season began, I made a conscious decision to prioritize healing and spend more time in nature. One afternoon, just days before my trip to Sedona for an inner child retreat, I went hunting with my dad. That day, I harvested my first bear with my crossbow. I was over the moon with excitement!

When I took the bear to the taxidermist, they asked what I wanted to do with it. Unsure, I listened to their suggestion of a bear skin rug and couldn't help but laugh—it was a small bear, only 57 pounds. I joked that the rug might just cover my arm! What I didn't know then was that this bear would play a pivotal role in uncovering a missing part of myself.

The next day, I had a meeting with one of my mentors. As I shared my bear story and my excitement for the retreat, I admitted that I felt weighed down—like I was dragging a heavy chain. My mentor asked, "What's on the other end of the chain?" I had no answer. He explained that my Native American guides wanted to help me discover what was at the other end of that chain.

In a powerful visualization session, I saw myself pulling up that heavy chain, revealing my three- or four-year-old self trapped in a cage. The emotions overwhelmed me. My guides helped me free her, and she introduced herself as "Little." I watched as she danced joyfully around a campfire, hand in hand with my guides. One of them draped a bear skin cape over her shoulders, with the bear's head as a hood.

That moment was profound. The bear I had harvested was meant for her. Tears streamed down my face as I watched "Little" dance, feeling joy and freedom for the first time. In that instant, everything clicked. The missing puzzle piece "Little" was found, and for the first time in a long time, I felt whole.

The emotions were overwhelming in the best way possible. I longed to return to the woods to ground myself in this newfound connection. Despite the work that awaited me, I promised myself that I'd return to nature the next morning to embrace these incredible feelings fully.

The following day, I woke to a crisp, bright morning and ventured into the woods. It turned out to be one of the most magical days I'd ever experienced. Squirrels and birds flitted about, deer chased each other, and every moment was alive with energy.

After two exhilarating hours of observing nature, the opportunity came to harvest my buck with my bow. I was, yet again, on cloud nine. I called my dad, who was hunting in another area, to share the incredible news. He came to help me retrieve the deer and celebrate with me.

That morning in the woods, I finally understood what it meant to just be. I wasn't thinking about what came next. I wasn't strategizing my life or my business. I was simply there—breathing, feeling, existing. The rustling leaves, the crisp morning air, the quiet hum of the earth beneath me—I let it all wash over me. And at that moment, for the first time in years, I felt whole. I wasn't searching for anything. I wasn't lost. I was home—within myself. That vibrational high from that day stuck with me for days as I awaited my next adventure to Sedona, Arizona.

Reclaiming My Truth

Two days later, I found myself in a place with an undeniable energetic pull, unlike anything I had ever felt before. As I arrived at the Airbnb, excitement and anticipation filled the air. I was about to embark on an inner child retreat with two of my amazing mentors, Tami and Zoe, and four other participants. Little did I know, this experience would change me forever.

Although I had never met any of the other participants before, their presence immediately made me feel safe, supported, and understood. What set my journey apart was that I was already reconnected with "Little," my inner child, who was by my side from the start. This was a unique foundation compared to the others, and it allowed me to dive deeper into the experience.

Tami and Zoe guided me through this retreat, helping me peel back the layers of limiting beliefs and fears that were keeping me stuck. What I discovered over the course of these days was nothing short of life-changing: I am multifaceted and possess many gifts. I have the ability to connect with those who have passed, I can move energy—not just within myself, but for others as well—beyond the traditional energy practices. Then, there's "Little," whose presence brings a unique and powerful magic all its own.

While many of these abilities are still unfolding, one thing became clear during this retreat: I've gained a profound clarity about aligning with my true self and embracing my life's purpose. This journey wasn't just about healing—it was about stepping into the full essence of who I am meant to be and that I need to utilize my gifts for the higher good.

Embracing Transformation: Unlocking Your Mind, Body, and Spirit Breakthrough

The journey of transformation is never easy, but it's always worth it. The unknown is uncomfortable, and fear often holds us back. But as I took those first steps, I discovered something powerful: The impossible starts to feel achievable when you choose to move forward. My role as a coach isn't to fix you; it's to guide you, to shine a light through the darkness so you can find your way. Together, we'll uncover the parts of you that need healing and alignment, allowing you to step into your highest self.

If my story resonates with you—if you're done feeling stuck and ready to step into your next level, I want you to know you don't have to do this alone. You are powerful, and your transformation is waiting. It starts with one decision. Scan the QR code below, and let's create a life that feels fully aligned, deeply fulfilling, and uniquely yours.

Stephanie Myers

Myers Consulting Group LLC
Gender Bias Strategist and Coach

https://www.facebook.com/stephanie.myers.182940/
https://www.instagram.com/biasbreakingbeauty/
https://stephaniemyers.org/
https://www.biasbreakingbeauty.com/

Stephanie Myers is a passionate advocate with over 20 years of experience in male-dominated industries. Inspired by her mother, Mary—a strong, capable woman—Stephanie grew up valuing individuality and self-worth beyond societal norms. These principles shaped her mission to challenge biases and help women excel in their careers. A global advocate for gender equity, Stephanie emphasizes the importance of confronting workplace biases that hinder women's success. Through her work, she demonstrates that women can achieve their goals and deserve equal recognition, pay, and opportunities. Stephanie furthers her mission through books, coaching, consulting, and speaking engagements that spark action and inspire change. Her vision is a world where success is based on character, not gender. Stephanie empowers women to claim their value, demand equality, and create inclusive environments where everyone can thrive. Her efforts aim to redefine leadership and break down barriers for future generations.

TODAY, WE LIVE

By Stephanie Myers

The world of mental health can seem open and vast to many and yet appear closed and very streamlined to others. Where your journey with mental illness places you on the spectrum often decides how you come to view this type of environment. While I have never thought of seeking out a therapist, counselor, or doctor to help one manage their thoughts and/or behaviors to be a bad and shameful thing, it did occur to me how so many will forgo help so as not to be labeled 'crazy or disturbed.' I appreciate more than ever the celebrities who used their platforms to take a mental break from their responsibilities to get their health back in balance. Oftentimes, seeing others get help encourages those who need it to seek help, too.

Hello, everyone! My name is Stephanie Myers. I am an empowerment coach and gender bias disruptor. Essentially, I teach women how to navigate gender bias in the workplace. More importantly, gender bias is a continuing fight more women still have to contend with today. A fight for gender equity that women will ultimately win.

I have worked in various male-dominated occupations in the last 25 years and experienced bias firsthand. There were times I tried to just ignore it (especially if it was very subtle), times I should have spoken up but didn't because I was woefully outnumbered gender-wise and feared the backlash, and lastly, the feeling of being isolated, believing that upper management would not be there to help (company culture and all).

Some of you may be asking… "What does challenging gender bias in the workplace have to do with anything mental?" Translation: "What does challenging gender bias have to do with feelings of isolation and being unseen, unheard, and undervalued in your life?" I'm happy to tell you, so let's begin.

My Beginning

I was born in 1966 in a small southern town in Tennessee. Needless to say, men and women had their assigned roles to play in the home and society. Both of my parents worked. My dad worked outside the home, and my mother spent days ironing other people's clothes until she got a job working outside the home when their children were all able to attend Head Start.

I was unaware as a child of the role gender bias played in the lives of every woman that I knew or to what extent such bias, teamed with outright racism, would play in my own life moving forward. A large part of my childhood that I do remember is my mother and how she was never satisfied with just being a wife and mother. While she never talked about it a lot, my mother always stressed the need for a woman to be her own person. She repeated the importance of not settling for less than you were worth and, if nothing else, standing up for yourself because there may never be someone to stand up for you! I marvel at this now, but I remember how I just blew her words off as meaningless since it was not having an impact on my pre-teen and teenage life. Just like so many of us when we think back to something our parents once told us... "I should have paid better attention."

Once I entered the workforce at 18 years of age, I was so happy just to be making money that I seldom allowed bias to disturb my flow. If I didn't get a job, I never asked why. I simply moved on to the next application. I have always worked. Sure, some jobs are easier and nicer than others, but there comes a time in everyone's life when money is not just something to spend frivolously, it determines where one will live and how one will be paid to live there. At that point, money and how much of it a person makes becomes very important.

Earlier, I stated that I have worked in various male-dominated occupations. The reason behind this was monetary. Most jobs within these industries pay more money. Simple economics. If I am going to work then why not make the most money I can get? These jobs were exciting yet very biased-laden in their performance and standards. Now you have my attention... my full attention.

Perception Is Everything

Can a woman do a man's job? That's a loaded question that depends on the type of job being considered and who it is you are asking the question. I have never considered any job as "a man's." Granted, millions of women are not interested in being firefighters, Formula One race car drivers, or serving in the military. But what about all the millions of women who desire to become (and are more than qualified) to become Fortune 500 CEOs, engineers, IT specialists, construction workers, or similar skilled trades? What's the reservation or hesitancy with women working in these jobs? Let me be clear on where I stand on work, specifically women and work. The best person that can do the job is the best person for the job, period, full stop. I do not believe that men are the best candidates for a job every time or all the time. It is this belief, combined with my past experiences with bias, that has led me to become the bias disruptor that I am today. Now, let's discuss how becoming a bias disruptor disrupted my own life for a short time.

Disruption

When I look back over my work history, I see how and to what degree bias shaped my view. I was then allowed to learn how bias has attempted to hinder or stop the goals of other women. This combination made me into the woman you are reading about today.

Challenging bias in the workplace has been meaningful to me, but things that matter often have a price attached to them. The price that I paid changed my entire life. It was during this time that I began questioning my effectiveness in fighting against the bias that I was experiencing at the time. Every woman has her own lived experience in life that she can choose to share or keep silent about. I choose to share mine in the hope that someone will realize no matter how you feel today, do not allow the darkness that surrounds you to make you feel as if there will never be light in your life again.

Being considered mentally ill runs the gamut, depending on who you talk to. Some people are still under the belief that if you seek out help and go talk to someone concerning your issue, that means you're unstable as an individual. Others think little of it and support people getting the help they need. I suppose it is up to your insurance coverage that ultimately determines the type of care a person receives. I knew I needed help. I knew talking to someone that I did not know and vice versa would help me in determining the way I would look at my life, my work, and what mattered to me the most in life from now until the day I die. I was right. I recently read a quote that stated:

"It's okay to disappear until you feel like you again." – Unknown

That quote sums up how I look at the time spent caring for myself. I disappeared until I was stronger in the fight. Now that I have returned, I'm unstoppable.

It's essential to understand the complexities surrounding gender bias. Gender bias is not just a workplace issue; it's a societal problem that shapes perceptions and behaviors. Women often contend with stereotypes that assert us as being less competent, less dedicated, and less capable of leadership roles simply because of our gender. This statement has caused problems for me specifically because there have been times throughout my work history where the stereotype of not having the "right look" for the position, or my favorite excuse, "A woman has never held this job before," as to why I was not chosen for the position. In my capacity as a bias disruptor and coach, I encourage women to take the necessary time to mentally heal from the negativity and the "No's" that are often heard, not because a better candidate or solution was chosen but because bias won the day!

Have you ever advised someone that you knew you needed to heed yourself? My time spent talking with a therapist was a wake-up call for me, shouting that I had not given enough time and attention to my mental state of mind. While I thought that I had everything under control (it's amazing how if you don't keep a watchful eye on "control," it will slip away from you), I now see how that control was like water slipping from between my fingers. Looking back, it all started as a minor frustration. Okay, there was more than one, so frustrations. Yes, I could feel myself getting tense because my neck would begin to feel like it had a slight crick in it. All of this was due to the frustration of not being seen, heard, or valued in a small corner of my life that I liked. I love my life, but what does a person do when life seems not to care or have any concern for you?

Unchecked frustration can lead to awful things happening to one's mind and, eventually, one's body. I absorbed all the frustration (along with the tension that came with it) and harbored it all within my mind and body. I had a major setback that made me question the type of women empowerment/bias-disrupting coach I was willing to be. Hey, if I was having a difficult time breaking through and challenging bias in my workplace, how was I ever going to help other women challenge bias and win? Winning means you are considered an equal member with all the rights, privileges, opportunities, and cash without being defeated simply because you are a woman. Defeat can be made to feel like a kiss of death, depending on the culture that you work in. It hurt because, up until now, I truly believed that progress was being made. Progress was made until "Goliath" entered the room.

Goliath

I refer to anything that presents itself as a major stumbling block in life as a Goliath. The harder you try to move Goliath out of your way, the more Goliath is determined to stay. The Goliath that appeared before me then, I had never encountered before, at least not to my recollection and not with such destruction permeating the air.

Remember, bias is not solely a systemic destroyer of a person's dreams and aspirations…it's a societal problem too. That's what I refused at the time to address, the societal side of my dilemma.

I know for certain that I did not take the bias that stood against me during this time seriously. I did not take it seriously because it came from people that I considered true colleagues. Years I have spent working with this select group of people. We knew one another…or so I thought. Somewhere and at some point, the tide in our working relationship changed, and I had not noticed until it was too late.

Relationships

Relationships between humans are a thing of wonder and a thing for intense scrutiny and study. I have never been married, yet I have always found it fascinating the relationship a man has with a woman and vice versa. We have witnessed married couples who have stayed together (and not just for the kids or the money) who truly care, support, and love each other. They have been married for years and years and years. Flip over the other side of the pancake, and we have witnessed couples who couldn't wait to get divorced, speak downright outrageous to one another (if they can speak to one another at all), and you are left wondering how they once claimed to love, honor, and cherish each other till death do us part. Now, that's dealing with love and not love.

Work relationships don't deal with love, but as time passes and days turn into months and months into years, you're able to get a sense of what a colleague is about. What kind of person are you dealing with?

Is respect a mutual thing shared amongst coworkers? Is hostility the agenda that commands center stage each day? What are you working with? I have always prided myself on having the ability to "read the room." It does not take me long to see who is kind or shy and who is condescending and extremely judgemental even though he or she pretends not to be. We (humans) are a particularly interesting species to study.

Sea Change

As I mentioned earlier, the tide shifted and I hadn't even noticed until I ran head-first into my Goliath. Bias can be very tricky when not explicit. Its subtlety can go unnoticed among nice, well-behaved individuals. Of course, a cry for "HELP" would rally the troops in support of me. I knew what bias looked and smelled like, yet I found myself hesitant to call it out because I was amongst people I knew and who knew me. We had worked together for years and seen others come and go, but we remained faithful and true. Let me take a second and third look at this again to make certain what I am witnessing is correct. It's logical not to want to face what you know is true when it is with people that you truly like...or at least this is what I told myself.

For the record and to the best of my knowledge, my experiences with gender bias have overwhelmingly come from men. Men who secretly questioned their own leadership capabilities, colleagues who desired someone (especially a woman) to whom they could bark orders and instill fear, or who never wanted what they said or done questioned by anyone. This is not an exhaustive list of the types of bias that can come your way, but these few examples give insight into what I (or any other woman) often contend with when working in male-dominated environments. Those biases and the actions required to resolve them were nothing new for me as I was quite familiar with them and knew how to work against them leading to not only my empowerment but the empowerment of women affected by the same situations. What undercut me and pulled the rug out from under my feet was the presence of women, women who I believed shared in my fight against bias in the workplace, fellow soldiers on our way toward gender equality, that caused the most pain and anxiety. Not bias from men but bias from women.

Matthew 10:36

"A person's enemies will be members of his own household."

Yes, this passage of scripture deals with family members and their betrayal or lack of loyalty towards one another, but it was the first thought that hit my mind once I realized how my sisters-in-arms had turned against me. To give context, these were women that I worked with for years, attended women empowerment meetings together, and signaled to our male co-workers that bias would not be tolerated against us or any female. We would gladly show them examples of what bias looked like in the workplace and how they could help to root it out. We were sisters…until we weren't. We held all positions within the company, from supervisor and department head, to rank-and-file personnel. It takes a village to combat bias and a village we were creating in the workplace. Apart from a village, we first became a sisterhood with shared beliefs and experiences surrounding the biases each of us had to contend with, past and present. This backstabbing didn't just happen in a vacuum. There was a repeated pattern of being unseen, unheard, and undervalued that lasted six months before I had to disappear, aka seek mental help advice, for how I was feeling.

How was I feeling, and what was the fallout? Here's the shortlist:

1. Feelings of Betrayal:

- I felt a deep sense of betrayal when experiencing bias from fellow women who I expected to support me.

2. Self-Doubt:

- The actions of a biased female led to diminished self-esteem, I began to internalize negative stereotypes and questioned my abilities and worth.

3. Isolation:

- Experiencing bias from other women led to feelings of loneliness and disconnection, especially when my larger work environment was unsupportive or hostile.

4. Reduced Trust:

- I became wary of trusting other women. I began limiting support systems and collaboration opportunities.

5. Anxiety and Stress:

- There was this ongoing fear of continued bias and retaliation, which heightened my anxiety levels, impacting my overall mental health and workplace performance.

6. Burnout:

- Dealing with the emotional toll of bias can contribute to my burnout because I felt unsupported and overextended.

7. Imposter Syndrome:

- As mentioned earlier in my writing, I began to doubt my accomplishments (which were significant) due to ongoing discrimination.

I am at a low point in my life during this time. I felt weak and I know that I am a strong woman! What is going on? What in the hell is happening to my mind and my body? What I have not shared with you is the physical toll this journey has cost me. Being on an emotional roller coaster is bad enough. Still, the added burden of bodily breakdown and the financial cost to heal me made this entire situation feel like I was traveling on the road to perdition. I thank God for doctors who work with the mind and the body. Even taking vacations to de-stress (I tried it) is sometimes not enough to handle what a person is dealing with at work. You can never run away from anything that has to be faced head-on.

My commitment toward further advancement and equality for women is greater now than ever before. As women continue to outpace men in gaining degrees and starting businesses, there seems to be a growing tide of resentment toward female empowerment. This is nothing new, of course, but it does make the struggle for full equality within society that much harder to attain. It is one thing for people to say they are in favor of civil rights for women. It is a completely different thing to put into practice and policy the needed legislation to make mere words a reality.

My concern for other women stems from the concern I had about myself and my journey to getting back to normal. The anxiety, mixed with bouts of depression, frustration, burnout, and sheer mental exhaustion, is now cast upon the waters, never to return again because I realize the self-care I was telling other women to maintain, I had neglected to do for myself. In my resolve to not report my colleagues (the sisterhood, you know), I allowed my mind and body to turn against itself. That was a terrible choice and one not to be repeated. I can admit this now. If my colleagues had been men, nothing would have stopped my reporting of the bias that I had experienced. Listening to a person is not hearing them. My colleagues listened to what I had to say, but they did not hear me at all. Isn't it amazing how you can talk to an individual, he or she can give you a response, yet the person never truly heard a word you said? Actions will always speak louder than words do, anyway. That is when you know the person did not hear your words. He or she can simply listen to you talk so that you can go away, and they can get on with more important things. Class dismissed.

Faith

It would be foolish of me to write my chapter and not speak about my faith. One of the driving forces behind my desire for empowerment is the need to rid our gender of the stereotypes that still plague women to this day. I find it insulting to believe that women are only good for birthing and housekeeping. To add insult to injury is the notion that men are the only gender who can make for great leaders, titans of industry, or spectacular innovators. Nonsense. As you and I very well know, women are capable of being anything they desire to be, so long as family, society, and the church do not try and talk them out of it! I once had a dear friend, a man, tell me that women are not good at making decisions because we get too emotional. I had to remind him that emotions are a good thing and that when Christ walked the Earth, He was emotional many times during his thirty-three years.

The hope and inspiration I feel right now (in spite of distractions and determinations that try and set us back), I want to share with all people but especially women. Our struggle to gain full acceptance as equal members of society has had its ebbs and flows, highs and lows. It has been my faith in Christ alone that has seen me through each battle for the win! Please don't misunderstand my motive here. I am not trying to win a soul to Christ or preach religion to anyone. I am only sharing how I have made it through some of the most difficult times (mentally and physically) in my life. I didn't do it alone. I would not have survived without an inner peace that eased the pain. When life hands you over-ripe lemons, you have to do more than think about making lemonade. You can't. The taste is not the same. You're better off making yourself a candle by hollowing out the over-ripe lemon and pouring in melted wax (use a wick). As the candle burns, you begin to smell a gentle, citrusy fragrance that will change your mood to a pleasant and relaxed state of being. My point? There will be times when going in the same direction and doing things like they have always been done will not work. You will reach your destination and achieve your goal through other means. Be ready for change. It is possible to reach your destination sooner and achieve your goal faster, but when obstacles like systemic biases stand in your way, ladies, the concern is not how fast just ensure that you keep moving forward. We are now in that time where it is not about speed but moving forward with our progress. Setbacks occur. Giving up and giving in to biased thinking and biased actions is no longer an option. Your silence is no longer a strategy.

One of the most important ways to keep us moving forward is our unity and collective strength. Women are more powerful and empowered when we share our stories of triumphs and defeats. Iron sharpens iron and we learn from one another best practices when experiencing bias. There is also the added benefit of no woman feeling like she is alone when dealing with bias and unity makes other women aware of the signs and tactics that bias will use to demean, dismiss, and discourage them from achieving their dreams. There truly is strength in numbers.

To address the naysayers who will read this chapter and still profess that nothing will change or it has gone as far as it can go (this whole women empowerment thing), all I have to say is "just watch." Time reveals many things. While some of us await the United States' first woman president, other nations have realized it sooner and have acted accordingly. In the rarified air of women ascending to the highest pinnacles of power, their vision and fortitude have inspired waves of progress and change. These women have dared to dream and then set out to achieve their dreams! Nothing, not even bias, can stop the inevitable wave of female innovation that is emerging across the globe. I hope that we can all celebrate the strides women have made, not get hung up on the setbacks that are sure to come, and continue to dream of a future where all voices are heard in governance. This is something the masses will have to face, and their denial will not hold up... Some women are natural leaders at birth.

We are relentless! When women are determined to succeed despite systemic and societal biases due to our gender, the forces that are attempting to stop or limit our progress know they will fail in the end. This is why it remains vital that all of us stay in the war for women's empowerment. We accept "full equality, full equity, and full transparency" in gaining the best jobs and positions, getting the same perks (like equal pay), along with the acknowledgment of our contributions just like a man. Nothing more, nothing less. Top leadership positions belong to the best candidate and gender is put to the side, if it is viewed at all!

It seems that as women take two steps forward in our empowerment, we are presently being dragged four steps back. Now is the time to confront bias, and we will keep the pressure coming until we WIN!

Most of us need better strategies to contend with the various weapons being used against us. That's where I step in to help. Your job, your business, your dream will not be squashed underfoot because you were born female. I am relentless in my pursuit of women's rights.

Let our voices be heard from every rural town to major city. Governmental policies and better business practices will reflect our resilience not to remain on the sideline as an afterthought. The entire women's history of fighting for justice and equality will not be erased from public memory.

If I reflect back and remember how down I was about myself, my job, and my purpose of helping women to advance and challenge gender bias, then compare myself to the way I currently see things, the paradigm shift occurred, and it was huge!

Our future is bright, but the brightest light shines for those generations of girls who will not have to wage war to have their brilliance noticed and respected.

Keep the unity of faith where women prevail and have access to whatever we are capable of achieving. "Onward and Upward" ladies! We are women, after all!

Conclusion

Everything that people find to be important has generally had an expensive price tag attached to it. Civil rights have always come at a cost to the people whose desire is to be free. I want to be free to make my own choices, to be appreciated for my work the same as my colleagues, not to mention getting equal pay for equal work. A better question to ask would be, why is society (and, by extension, the organizations women work for) still trying to deny millions of us our rightful place in the world?

Let's chat. I'm here to help because Today, We Live!

Sonia Rodrigues

Transition to Wellness
Psychotherapist & Life Transition Coach

https://www.linkedin.com/in/sonia-rodrigues-48b87149/
https://www.facebook.com/SoniaRodriguesLPC/
https://instagram.com/transition.to.wellness
http://www.transitiontowellness.com/
https://soniarodrigues-marto.tribesites.com/

Sonia Rodrigues has been a licensed psychotherapist for over 20 years. She is the owner of a psychotherapy and coaching practice called Transition to Wellness. She has worked with people of all ages, helping them navigate various challenges in their life. She utilizes a holistic approach and provides a safe and supportive environment where her clients can feel supported on their path towards healing from their traumatic experiences and guided towards creating the life they desire. She provides individual therapy, coaching and also offers a variety of workshops on topics related to trauma, post-traumatic growth and fostering resilience.

From Struggle to Strength: Embracing the Journey with Compassion & Self-Care

By Sonia Rodrigues

There are moments in life when everything feels heavy. When the weight of our thoughts, our responsibilities, and the world itself can feel like it is pressing down on us all at once. And if you are anything like most women I know, you have probably found yourself in those dark spaces where it feels like there is no way out or that you are just encountering one obstacle after another and cannot catch your breath. It is in those moments when self-doubt creeps in, when anxiety whispers in your ear, or when depression settles in like an unwelcome guest causing you to feel like you are at a complete standstill in your life. These are the times when you feel scared, lost, and so very alone. It is okay to feel this way when life has thrown you curveballs. Allow yourself to be vulnerable, to be *human*—because everyone goes through moments of distress and hardship.

The Power of Vulnerability

The journey from struggle to strength is not one of smooth, effortless steps, nor is it a linear process. Sometimes, it feels like two steps forward and one step back. But even in those setbacks, there's beauty. There's growth. And though it can feel impossible in the moment, embracing that journey with compassion for yourself is where the real strength lies.

True strength is not about being unbreakable. It is not about wearing a perfect smile when you feel like the world is falling apart. It's about showing up for yourself, even on days when it feels like you have nothing left to give. It's about letting yourself rest when you need it. It's about acknowledging that you're struggling without shaming yourself for it. And most importantly, it's about not letting yourself stay in isolation, even though that's often the place we gravitate to when things get tough.

I understand how easy it can be to retreat into yourself when you're facing hard times. The urge to hide, to close the door, and to shut out the world, can feel so overwhelming. And maybe, just maybe, you feel like no one would understand, or you fear being a burden to others. But I want to gently remind you: You *don't* have to carry it all alone. You don't have to be the strong one all the time. In fact, there is immense strength in asking for help, in sharing your truth with someone who will listen, and in showing your vulnerability. It's through those honest, raw moments that you will find connection—and connection is where healing happens.

The Power of Connection

You deserve to lean on others when you're struggling. We *all* do. No one should have to go through hardship alone. The courage to reach out and share your feelings, even if it is just with one person who you trust, can be life-changing. It can create a space where you can breathe a little easier, knowing someone else understands what you are experiencing. When you show up as your true self, you give others permission to do the same. You become a light for those around you, a quiet reminder that they are not alone in their pain.

And in those moments when you are both the listener and the one reaching out, there is a kind of magic that happens. When you reach out, you help others feel seen and heard, and that is where healing truly begins. The connection we build in our vulnerability is what reminds us that we are not defined by our struggles but by the strength it takes to keep going...one step at a time, or one at a time.

Self-care is another act of compassion we too often forget about. It's not just about lighting a candle or taking a walk (though those things are wonderful!). True self-care is much deeper—it's the act of treating yourself with the same kindness and grace you would show to a friend. It's giving yourself permission to pause when you need to. It's listening to your heart and soul, and knowing when to take a break, to rest, or to ask for support. It is honoring your feelings and accepting that it is okay to not be okay sometimes. It is about giving yourself room to breathe, and not judging yourself for it.

I know it can feel like the world wants you to be strong in a way that looks flawless, like you should always have it together. But let me remind you of something: *real* strength is in your ability to lean into your feelings, to be honest with yourself, and to share your truth with others. It is in those moments of sharing, of reaching out and saying, "I need help" or "I don't have all the answers," that you become stronger than you realize. This vulnerability also leads to powerful connections with others.

Vulnerability has a profound power to connect us with others, especially when we share our struggles and emotions openly. When we allow ourselves to be vulnerable, we give others the opportunity to see our true selves—without the masks we often wear to protect ourselves from judgment. This openness creates a space for shared experiences, where others can relate to our pain, fears, and doubts. As we realize that we are not alone in our feelings, we experience the comfort of knowing someone else understands. This connection brings a sense of support and belonging, and in turn, fosters our own healing. When we share our vulnerabilities, we not only offer a shoulder for others to lean on but also find healing in the compassion and empathy that flows both ways. It is through these authentic, shared moments that we truly grow and heal together.

Turning Our Struggles Into Opportunities for Learning and Growth

As a psychotherapist for over twenty years, I have been blessed to work with women who have faced various challenges and obstacles in their lives. I feel even more blessed that they trusted me to open up about these struggles and to share their stories. Over the years, what I have learned is that life does not always go as planned, and the vision of what we want things to look like can often change within the blink of an eye. I have learned that trauma, grief, loss, and illness can debilitate anyone regardless of how successful they are or how much money they have. Hardships show up for everyone at some point in their lives. Experiencing unexpected hardships can completely throw us off balance and send us into a tailspin at times. They can keep us from meeting our goals on time or allow us to feel stuck, lonely, or depressed. One of the ways we can get through is to remind ourselves that everyone experiences hardships at varying times in their lives and that these hardships can often be viewed as opportunities for learning and growth. Our challenges will often lead us in directions we would have never imagined. When we are experiencing hardships, what is most important is to find the right support and connections, so you do not feel alone on your journey. Chances are that there is someone out there who may have experienced something similar or may have knowledge of different ways in which you could navigate the challenge you are currently experiencing. Seek them out whenever possible.

Other things that are helpful when you experience difficulties in your life include treating yourself with self-compassion, taking time to rest and care for yourself, focusing on various dimensions of wellness that heal your mind, body, and soul, and reminding yourself that you are resourceful and will figure out how to navigate it with the right support, connections, and resources. Another important thing to consider is that it takes time to heal and recover and that there is no specific time frame for healing; it takes you as long as you need, try not to judge yourself for taking the time you need to work through challenges. Be kind to yourself and recognize that healing can look different for everyone. What you need is not what someone else might need. Focus on what you need to recover and try out different strategies or techniques for coping until you find what works best for you. Healing is not linear, there will be lots of ups and downs, and that is normal. Things may trigger you years later when you think you have put it all behind you. This is all normal and part of the recovery process. Take the time to reflect on what happened, how it makes you feel, identify what it means for you and if there is a lesson to learn. You will be stronger because of everything you have ensured. You may not feel strong in the moment you are experiencing the hardships, but when you take the time to fully heal and integrate your healing process into your journey of growth and personal development, you will certainly experience strength and empowerment.

In my work as a therapist, I have supported many women through some very difficult situations. What I have noticed is that those who have sought out support have been able to recover faster. I cannot emphasize enough the power of connection during moments of hardship; it can be a powerful resource. When terrible things happen to us, it can feel like the best thing to do is to isolate ourselves in feelings of shame. That is understandable but can serve as a disservice to your healing. We live in a world that allows for anonymity in our outreaches of need, but be sure to remind yourself that everyone experiences some sort of struggle in their lives, and there is likely someone out there you can reach out to for support. At a minimum, you can reach out to free online resources via phone, video, text, or chat, or you can read articles or blogs on how to cope with what you are experiencing. Just find some sort of support to help you through.

Embracing the Unexpected: Practical Tools for Overcoming Life's Challenges

While it is hard to prepare for the unknown or the unexpected, here are a few things you can do when this happens:

1. Accept that challenges and obstacles will show up, and we have limited control over when they do show up or how they show up.

2. Have faith and confidence in your ability to figure things out when you need to and to find the support and necessary resources you need to overcome the challenges or obstacles that show up.

3. Be proactive in your approach to ensuring you create a healthy work-life balance.

4. Identify different coping skills you can use when faced with hardships and create your own personal coping "toolbox" that you can use when you need support with coping with these obstacles.

5. Integrate daily self-compassion and self-care practices into your life that nourish your mind, body, and soul, which will aid in fostering the resilience you need to overcome challenges.

6. Focus on what you can control and try not to fixate on what feels out of control; you can control how you respond to hardships and what you choose to do to overcome them.

You are a woman of incredible strength, even when you don't feel it. Your resilience isn't about powering through without pause—it's about having the courage to feel everything, the hard stuff and the good stuff. It's about asking for help, it's about offering a listening ear, and it's about showing up for yourself even when the world feels too heavy. You are stronger than you know, and you are *not* defined by the struggles you face.

If there's one thing I want you to carry with you from this chapter, it's this: It's okay to not be okay. It's okay to ask for help. It's okay to lean on others. And it's okay to take the time you need to heal. Your journey, with all its bumps, bruises, and moments of grace, is what makes you who you are. And that woman? She is resilient. She is compassionate. And she is worthy of all the love, care, and support that life has to offer.

So, let's walk this journey together. Let's be kind to ourselves and to one another. Let's share our stories, and in doing so, create a community where we can all heal and grow. You are not alone. You never have to be.

Summary

In this chapter, we explored the deep human experience of facing struggles, feeling lost, and being overwhelmed by the weight of life's challenges. We acknowledged that it's okay to feel vulnerable and to admit when we are struggling because it's through this vulnerability that we find true strength. Rather than retreating into isolation, we learned that vulnerability allows us to connect with others, creating bonds of support that foster healing. We are reminded that healing is not a linear process, and it's essential to approach our journey with compassion and patience. By treating ourselves with kindness, seeking support, and honoring our unique path to recovery, we allow ourselves to grow and learn from life's obstacles. Most importantly, we discovered that we are not defined by our struggles, but by the resilience we show in overcoming them. Our shared experiences create powerful connections, and when we come together, we create a community of support where we can all heal and thrive. You are strong, you are worthy, and you are never alone.

Final Thoughts

As we close this chapter, I want to remind you that you are not defined by your struggles, but by the strength and resilience you summon to navigate them. The journey through life's challenges is not about avoiding hardship, it is about learning how to rise and grow from our past experiences. It is about embracing your vulnerability, knowing it is okay not to have it all together, and understanding that reaching out for help is a powerful form of strength.

You are worthy of love, care, and support, especially in your toughest moments. Remember that healing does not happen overnight, and it does not look the same for everyone, so try not to judge yourself for taking longer than others to heal and move on, we are all different in how we process emotions Be patient with yourself, and do not hesitate to lean on the people around you or seek out resources that can guide you through your most challenging times. There is immense power in connection, whether it is sharing your own story or simply being there for someone else. We are all walking this journey together, and through compassion, vulnerability, and support, we can find healing and growth.

I would like to share these national resources for you in the hopes they can either provide some support during difficult moments for yourself or for someone else:

National Alliance on Mental Illness (NAMI)
Website: https://www.nami.org
Helpline: 1-800-950-NAMI (1-800-950-6264)

NAMI is a leading mental health organization in the U.S., offering support, education, and advocacy for individuals experiencing mental health challenges. They have resources for coping with stress, anxiety, depression, and other mental health conditions. NAMI offers online resources, peer support groups, and a helpline for people seeking mental health support and information.

The National Suicide Prevention Lifeline (988 Suicide & Crisis Lifeline)
Website: https://988lifeline.org
Phone: Dial 988

The 988 Lifeline is a 24/7 service that provides free and confidential support for anyone experiencing a mental health crisis, including thoughts of suicide. This resource connects individuals to trained counselors who can provide immediate support and connect them to local services. The lifeline is available for people in emotional distress or experiencing thoughts of self-harm.

Women's Health Network (WHN) – Trauma and Recovery Support
Website: https://www.womenshealth.gov

WHN offers a wide range of information on mental, physical, and emotional health specifically geared toward women. They provide resources on coping with trauma, managing stress, and recovery. Their content includes support for dealing with anxiety, depression, and other mental health challenges often experienced by women as they navigate various life transitions and difficulties.

JOIN THE MOVEMENT!
#BAUW

Becoming An Unstoppable Woman
With She Rises Studios

She Rises Studios was founded by Hanna Olivas and Adriana Luna Carlos, the mother-daughter duo, in mid-2020 as they saw a need to help empower women worldwide. They are the podcast hosts of the *She Rises Studios Podcast* and Amazon best-selling authors and motivational speakers who travel the world. Hanna and Adriana are the movement creators of #BAUW - Becoming An Unstoppable Woman: The movement has been created to universally impact women of all ages, at whatever stage of life, to overcome insecurities, and adversities, and develop an unstoppable mindset. She Rises Studios educates, celebrates, and empowers women globally.

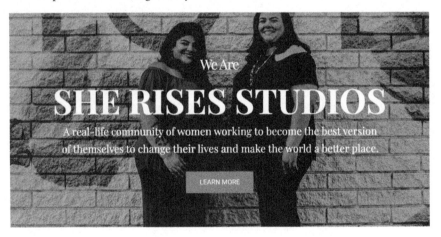

Looking to Join Us in our Next Anthology or Publish YOUR Own?

She Rises Studios Publishing offers full-service publishing, marketing, book tour, and campaign services. For more information, contact info@sherisesstudios.com

We are always looking for women who want to share their stories and expertise and feature their businesses on our podcasts, in our books, and in our magazines.

SEE WHAT WE DO

OUR PODCAST **OUR BOOKS** **OUR SERVICES**

Be featured in the Becoming An Unstoppable Woman magazine, published in 13 countries and sold in all major retailers. Get the visibility you need to LEVEL UP in your business!

Have your own TV show streamed across major platforms like Roku TV, Amazon Fire Stick, Apple TV and more!

Learn to leverage your expertise. Build your online presence and grow your audience with FENIX TV.
https://fenixtv.sherisesstudios.com/

Visit www.SheRisesStudios.com to see how YOU can join the #BAUW movement and help your community to achieve the UNSTOPPABLE mindset.

Have you checked out the *She Rises Studios Podcast?*

Find us on all MAJOR platforms: Spotify, IHeartRadio, Apple Podcasts, Google Podcasts, etc.

Looking to become a sponsor or build a partnership?

Email us at info@sherisesstudios.com

Made in the USA
Monee, IL
30 May 2025

18173469R00095